THE
FLIP
SIDE

THE
FLIP
SIDE

Break Free of the Behaviors
That Hold You Back

FLIP FLIPPEN

WITH DR. CHRIS J. WHITE

SPRINGBOARD PRESS

NEW YORK BOSTON

Springboard Press
Hachette Book Group USA
237 Park Avenue, New York, NY 10169
Visit our Web site at www.HachetteBookGroupUSA.com

First Edition: May 2007

Springboard Press is an imprint of Warner Books. The Springboard name and logo are trademarks of Hachette Book Group USA.

Library of Congress Cataloging-in-Publication Data
Flippen, Flip.
The flip side : break free of the behaviors that hold you back/Flip Flippen; with Chris J. White.—1st ed.
p.   cm.
Summary: "Learn how recognizing your biggest weakness can unleash your greatest strength in the first book by educator, business coach, and growth guru Flip Flippen"—Provided by the publisher.
ISBN 978-0-446-58078-6
1. Success—Psychological aspects.   2. Behavior modification.
I. White, Chris J., Dr.   II. Title.
BF637.S8F593 2007
158.1—dc22
2006036872

10 9 8 7 6 5 4 3 2 1

Q-FF

Printed in the United States of America

To my wife and my love, Susan.
Through you, my life is full, whole, and not yet finished.

Contents

PART III
Overcoming Personal Constraints

THE
FLIP
SIDE

Introduction

If I asked you *what one thing* determines your level of ultimate success, what would your answer be? Your talent? Your skills? A college degree?

Is it possible that something *other* than your talents, abilities, personality, or academic achievements will define how far you go in life? Could it be that the things that hold you back—or constrain you—are a far more reliable indicator of your success than any skills or talent you may possess? And if it is possible to identify whatever those personal constraints are and break free of them, do you believe that you could soar to new heights in your life? Would you choose to break free of your personal constraints if I could show you what and where they are and how they are affecting you? If you answered yes to these questions, then read on.

Physician, Heal Thyself

This book should have been finished several years ago.

And I think you'll find it fascinating why it wasn't. The various reasons all boiled down to one single source (drumroll, please)...

My personal constraints.

How ironic that the completion of a book about *your* personal constraints was being held back by *mine!* You see, I thrive when things are changing. I crave the energy I feel when I talk about and act on new ideas. I get bored easily, and the status quo wears me down.

When I don't seem to be making obvious, measurable progress, I have difficulty resisting the urge to change things to get moving— even if this means moving in a wrong direction!

So the progress of this book has stalled several times. I've replaced various people involved in the project. And, of course, I'm always changing the manuscript. I suspect (or at least hope!) that most of these changes were beneficial. But I also know that some of them slowed down the project unnecessarily.

I am not a better writer today than when I started years ago, nor am I smarter. The difference is that I found out which personal constraints were affecting my performance, then took the steps required to break free of them once and for all. Does it really work? You tell me:

- My company, The Flippen Group, is the largest teacher-educator company in North America.
- We are among the best executive-development companies in the nation.
- Tens of thousands of educators have experienced our processes, and millions of young people are impacted each year.
- Our ideas have been featured on the *Today* show, during the Super Bowl, and in numerous articles, dissertations, papers, and radio and news shows.
- Our staff continues to expand, teaching others in conferences and seminars the same key principles that brought and continue to take them to new levels in their own lives.

To become the best I can be means that I have to identify the things that are holding me back and take the steps to remove them from my life. I call those things personal constraints, and I want to show you how to find and remove yours—before *they* find *you*.

What defines The Flippen Group's success as individuals, and as a company, is that we work hard to identify not only our strengths but also those personal constraints that keep us from being what we can be, and then we do whatever it takes to break them. We have helped thousands of people Overcome Personal Constraints (OPC), and we have watched them win—in arenas from Wall Street to NASCAR to the Super Bowl to Best Superintendent to Greatest Mom.

Do you know your own most crippling personal constraints? Are you ready to deal with these obstacles to your success?

If so, join me and the thousands of others who have already gone before you to "the Flip side," by identifying and removing whatever is holding you back from wherever it is you have always wanted to go.

How to Use This Book

I take things personally.

I go after personal constraints, and I give everything I have to help my patients and clients, because the consequences of not dealing with them is personal.

Families implode. Careers derail. Relationships unravel. Personal constraints often act like hidden land mines, detonating where and when we least expect them.

The ideal situation for me would be to sit down with you in my office here in Texas to hear your story, help you understand the concept of Overcoming Personal Constraints (OPC), then diagnose and prescribe a step-by-step plan to help you break their hold in your life for good. Case closed.

Since I obviously can't do that in person for everyone, I felt that any book I wrote would have to be powerful enough to help the reader ultimately get to the same place. It needed to be *accurate* enough to diagnose the problem, *simple* enough to incorporate into a busy life, and the prescriptions *effective* enough to begin the process of change immediately.

That's what this book is designed to do. After thirty years of helping patients and clients find freedom from their most damaging behaviors, I've put all my findings together in one place—for *you*. This book will help you recognize and stop the self-sabotaging behaviors most of us struggle with on a daily basis. The process is proven, and it is the most personal, powerful approach you will experience to produce lasting change.

Chapters 1–4 introduce the concept of Understanding Personal Constraints and give an overview of the Top 10 Killer Constraints— the ten most damaging constraints that are true career and relationship busters and cause endless problems in everyday life. These constraints are examined individually in chapters 5–14 and are illustrated in true stories from my years of clinical, corporate, and education-system experience (the names of people and organizations have been changed in most cases). This section is designed to make you familiar with each constraint and able to recognize its presence in yourself and others—either by itself or in common constraint combinations. Some of the stories focus on the extreme end of a particular constraint because that is the most dangerous area, but be aware that you can have shades of a constraint that can still be damaging.

A Symptom Checklist within each constraint chapter helps you to "diagnose," or identify, which constraints are most problematic for you. Don't overanalyze your scores on these assessments, just use them to further reinforce which constraints seem to impact you the most. For example, you may have selected only three or four symptoms from a certain constraint, but as you looked over the suggested TrAction Steps, you saw some things you could do differently.

As you go through each of the checklists, you'll probably notice one or more constraints emerging as areas you struggle with the most. You may be tempted to skip those chapters that you believe do not impact you, but I encourage you to read each constraint chapter, since understanding how personal constraints operate in those around us is an important part of OPC. I even include a section at the end of each chapter that helps you understand how to better interact with someone who has that constraint.

Your top one or two killer constraints will be officially identified in chapter 15, and even if you discover you have several killer constraints, you will work on no more than two at a time. After you see visible, measurable change on the top one or two personal constraints that most impact you, then you can move on.

In chapter 15 you will also build your custom TrAction Plan, using the outline provided or a downloadable electronic version available at www.flipsidebook.com. It is recommended that you download the TrAction Plan for easy logging, e-mailing, and printing options.

As you start the process, you will need to think of two or three trusted friends, family members, or business associates who will support you as you bring your plan to life. From helping you identify your greatest strengths and most damaging constraints to giving you feedback in the accountability section, their input is a crucial and invaluable part of the process.

At the end of the book, I'll present some "where do I go from here?" options to help you make personal growth a lifestyle. But whether you use the book alone or choose to take additional steps, the TrAction Plan will help you dig in to begin a powerful tracking and feedback system. This will result in each targeted constraint being systematically broken and replaced with the behaviors needed for what you want to change *to*—that is, your specified behavioral goals.

Are you ready?

Then grab a cup of coffee and have a seat in my "office," because *change starts here.*

PART

I

*Understanding
Personal
Constraints*

1 SomethingIs Holding You Back

I learned everything I know from my clients. After seeing more than seventeen thousand patients through my practice as a psychotherapist and working with thousands of educators and many of the largest and most successful companies in the world, I had to learn *something*.

One thing I knew early on was that I wanted to spend my life helping people. After finishing graduate school I decided to work with underprivileged kids and street gangs, so I started an outpatient free clinic that served anyone who walked in the door. We were poor, but we were making a difference, and that was what mattered most. I started with an all-volunteer staff, then slowly added professionals to care for the more difficult needs that people brought to us.

Janice and Tony showed up within one week of each other at the clinic. They were both extremely likeable teenagers with a lot in common—they each came from dysfunctional, alcoholic families and grew up struggling to survive from day to day, well on the way to following in their families' footsteps. On the brink of destroying their lives before they had even begun, they enrolled for counseling.

Janice and Tony had more in common than just their backgrounds. They were energetic and curious about the world around them, demonstrating intellectual and creative abilities that had not been cultivated by the urban schools they attended. And they were both burdened by a profound lack of self-confidence—no surprise given the challenges they'd already faced, but heartbreaking nonetheless.

Ten years later Janice had completed college and law school and was working as a senior attorney at a university chancellor's office. Tony, on the other hand, was in prison on manslaughter charges stemming from a drug-related shoot-out.

Searching for the Keys

The question haunted me like no other.

What made the difference?

Why was Janice able to embrace the opportunities presented to her, while Tony could not escape the disadvantages? In my years at the clinic, I saw countless cases like Janice's and Tony's—people of comparable backgrounds and abilities who attained dramatically different levels of success.

Within a few years I found my clinic and my home (so much for the "outpatient" part) overflowing with kids carrying pain my textbooks had never mentioned. My graduate-school classes had introduced them as case studies for dissection and analysis, not as real, breathing, bleeding human beings.

Despite my dedication and noble intentions, not all of them turned the corner. I have cried more than I would have imagined when I think of what became of some of them. Several young men and women were murdered within the first year that I worked in the clinic. All of the deaths were drug related, and each story echoed many of the same issues.

Yet a lot of the kids coming to the clinic had great potential. Many have been able to do tremendous things with their lives, while others have known nothing but struggle and disappointment. Some overcame major obstacles, while others, in almost identical situations, perpetuated the cycles of self-destruction—their progress simply stopped, as if something insurmountable was holding them back.

For these kids the alternative to success was often prison, drug addiction, or even death. With the stakes that high, I couldn't stand by and watch them go down without a fight. I had to discover why their lives could go only so far—and what, if anything, I could do to help them make their lives better.

I started down the road that has been my life's journey for the past three and a half decades, and it turned out to be about much more than street kids and gang members. It turned out to be about business executives, and schoolteachers, and athletes, and *me*.

My work expanded quickly, putting me in regular contact with people who pursued excellence in a variety of fields—from salespeople trying to hit quotas to athletes trying to break world records—and their experiences revealed a common theme: *real success demands more than talent and ability.*

What is real success? It is far more than making money or getting to the top. It is about a person becoming EVERYTHING he or she can be. It's being a great son or daughter, parent, boss, or employee. It's becoming kind, and thoughtful, and taking initiative in life to make the world a better place. Being successful is being able to see past your private agenda and learning how to manage innate tendencies toward selfishness and greed to become more sensitive to others who share your journey.

Real success is being known as someone who improves the lives of those you touch—which also means that we strive to touch more because internally *we know that we can make a difference.*

So many people are only a fraction of what they can be, accomplishing so much less than their potential. They dream about doing more and being better, but something bigger than their talent seems to be holding them back with invisible ropes and heavy weights. I was driven to figure out what that "something" was. If I couldn't find out what held people back, how could I ever hope to help them?

Soon after I committed to searching for answers, the critical questions turned inward, and I had to ask myself what was holding *me* back. I looked at my life and saw plenty of room for improvement—as a father, husband, friend, business owner, entrepreneur, and human being. I realized that if I could overcome the things blocking me from fully using my abilities, I would be miles ahead in the game of living.

As the clinic grew to be one of the larger mental-health clinics in Texas, I learned the hard way that some parents didn't care much, if anything, about their kids. Many of the children we saw were homeless, or abused, or simply ignored as they tried so desperately to find their place in life. In 1988 our foundation built a five-hundred-acre boys' ranch and, later, a ranch for girls. To this day that work continues, and I never cease to be amazed at how the kids flourish in the presence of "family" and parental care.

Over the next few years, I had the opportunity to work with many corporate executives through the Center for Executive Development at Texas A&M University, in College Station, Texas, where I live. These invitations came because others were hearing of the difference we were making in the lives of young people. The interim president of Texas A&M, Dr. Dean Gage, wanted to expose our work and way of thinking to corporate executives around the country. It was a tremendous time of growth and intellectual challenge for all of us. For one thing I learned that many corporate executives are a lot like enthusiastic kids. In fact, in some cases I couldn't find any differences at all, other than age! So often they grappled with many of the same issues; they just called them by different names. For example, in school you can be labeled ADD or ADHD, but then as an adult you are called an entrepreneur. Interesting how that works, isn't it?

Growing Greatness

Meanwhile, my two boys were growing up, and I wanted them to do well, too. One night the boys got into an argument, and the next thing I knew, a lot of yelling was going on. When I confronted them about it, one of them said, "Well, he isn't doing what I told him to do!" And there you have it. The same thing I had heard a business executive say that very morning—*You're not doing what I told you to do!*—before he started yelling at his employees. Lack of self-control didn't work for Matthew and Micah, and it didn't work for the executive, either, who soon discovered he was approaching an unexpected career crisis. By addressing the issue with my boys early on, I was hedging my bets they would not be doing the same thing at forty years of age! As a parent I wanted my sons to be the best they could be, to play at the top of their game—not just in business, but in life. *I wanted to grow greatness in my children.*

Today they are partners in a thriving company they bought together. As they put it, "Pop, we are having the time of our life."

For several years I presented lectures to graduating seniors at Texas A&M. A typical presentation would start with a question. As I walked in I would ask, "Why are you here?" The response was a roomful of blank faces. Then a lone voice would invariably pipe up.

"Do you mean here at A&M, or here in the auditorium, or here on the earth? What are you talking about?"

"Here."

"To get a degree!"

"Why do you want a degree?"

"To get a job."

"Why do you want a job?"

"To buy a car!"

"Hmmm, let me see if I have this right. You came to Texas A&M four years ago and spent about one hundred thousand dollars so you could buy a car. *Is that right?*"

In that light the investment didn't seem like such a smart one.

Of course the next questions were the *real* ones: "What are you here for? What are your talents and gifts? What are your dreams? Why would you focus on a car rather than a purpose? What would happen if you lived your life to its fullest? *What could you become if you identified your greatest strengths and removed your worst constraints?*"

And that last question, my friend, is the question of your life.

I learned many years ago that it didn't matter how many hours I put in, or how hard I worked, I still couldn't get that much MORE out of my efforts. I was working as hard as I could at being my best, but I was still stuck. The growth I experienced was incremental—which was better than no growth at all—but it was not taking me where I wanted to go.

My clients and patients were being stifled by behaviors and thoughts that I believed they could and would change—if only they recognized them and the damage they were doing. They had plenty of talent and resources, but they let their attitudes and actions get in the way of using them. I also saw that specific behaviors were holding me back from becoming my best. I recognized the similarities between myself and other people who were struggling with their constraints: the distance runner who possessed great speed but lacked mental endurance, the promising junior executive who was too deferential to take charge, or the gifted young student who was simply too self-critical to see her true worth.

My goal was to identify the obstacles in our way and provide the skills to plow through them. I discovered that most limiting behaviors can be traced to a handful of distinct, measurable constraints. I began to develop strategies to release people from their constraints. This evolved into Overcoming Personal Constraints (OPC), the simple program I have used to help thousands of people from all walks of life.

Understanding the Secrets of Personal Success

Consider again the stories of Janice and Tony, the teenagers who arrived at the clinic facing such similar challenges. Working with our counselors they both exhibited what we've come to recognize as signs of low self-confidence, such as difficulty initiating action and making decisions, and periods of crippling self-doubt. But there was one big difference. Tony also demonstrated a lack of self-control that had a profoundly destructive impact because it was coupled with his anger. In his case the results were devastating: too impulsive to rein in his aggression, Tony got caught up with a violent, drug-dealing crowd and eventually landed in prison.

Janice, on the other hand, had enough self-control to stick with an action plan. Following the confidence-building steps mapped out by her counselor, she bonded with a group of other kids who were willing to be supportive and share their lives with her. Janice learned that she wasn't the only one with problems and that being vulnerable could ultimately empower her. As she practiced simple esteem-building skills such as making eye contact, affirming others, and allowing herself to relax and smile more often, her self-confidence began to increase. She recognized that her behaviors were compromising her potential, and she committed herself to working hard for the brighter future she now felt she deserved. With her self-confidence on the mend, Janice's natural abilities were finally able to blossom. In Janice's words, "I began to taste success, and I wanted more of it."

Two Diverging Roads

OPC is designed to help each of us enjoy the success that our self-defeating behaviors have hindered in our lives. Our personal constraints can define us only if we let them. When we ignore our constraints, we allow them to limit us; but when we identify and seek to overcome them, we dramatically improve our chances of success.

Daniel was a successful young executive with little ability to nurture others. About the time I began working with him, I was also hired to consult by a philanthropic organization run by a dynamic young executive named Peter. Interestingly, both men demonstrated remarkably similar strengths and constraints. Even though Peter ran a nonprofit organization, he had little desire to nurture others. How they handled their personal constraints, however, couldn't have been more different.

When I met with them individually, Daniel and Peter had the same reaction: each argued that his issues must not be that important or he wouldn't be so successful. In response I asked each man what he thought would happen if I brought in his wife or his closest associates. Would they agree with me? What would they say?

Daniel was quick to answer. "I guess they would tell you what I told them to tell you," he said jokingly.

Peter, on the other hand, was speechless, and as I watched him imagine the scenario, I could actually see tears well up in his eyes. "Oh, my gosh," he finally said, visibly struggling with the unpleasant realization of how others saw him. He looked at me with understanding. "I will change this," Peter said. "I promise."

That promise was the beginning of a wonderful new journey for Peter, and I was honored to lead him through each step of the process. First, he sat down with his top staff and asked for their honest feedback, resisting the impulse to argue, and requesting specific examples of any constraints that they agreed upon. He had deliberately planned the first meeting with his colleagues, rather than his wife, so he wouldn't be tempted to start a family argument. He came back with the examples they gave him, and we developed a personalized plan to address his constraints. He began to build affirming and nurturing behaviors into his life, giving genuinely supportive compliments to his staff and asking them how he could help them grow and be more successful.

Next, he asked his wife for her feedback. In response to her words, he made several changes. He cut out unnecessary travel, traded his golf weekends with his buddies for date nights with his wife, and committed to hugging her each time he left and returned. He chose his words more carefully, rather than giving in to his tendency to be critical, and began spending more time with his children. Within a few months he was back in my office with tears in his eyes once more—however, these were tears of joy. He told me the experience had changed his life. "Everything's different now. I'm in love with my wife, my children, and my life."

Daniel, however, has not fared so well. Rather than address his constraints, he instructed us to focus more on the people around him and in his organization. He knew that the people in the field, who didn't know him closely, would give a better report. They had such positive feelings about the organization's work that they felt good about Daniel, as well. But he didn't realize how little respect some of his key staff members had for him. As a result four of his top leaders have left the organization in the last year. As long as he can keep people coming up the ranks and filling in the slots, his organization will appear to be okay, but the constant departures are taking a toll on Daniel and on his firm. He is undermining his achievements by ignoring his constraints.

While everyone is on a life journey, not every traveler is willing to read the map to take the best route. You can choose to live life as you always have, or you can choose to identify and overcome what has held you back.

As a psychotherapist, I've learned what works—sometimes painfully. After seeing many thousands of patients over three and a half decades, building a nonprofit clinic and residential treatment facilities, building several successful privately held companies, having privileges at two psychiatric hospitals, and having clients that ranged from drug addicts to world-class athletes to corporate moguls running multinational companies, I've discovered five foundational principles that determine where a person goes with his or her life. I've also discovered the ten most deadly constraints that can absolutely destroy you if left unchecked.

2 The Foundations of OPC

I have always been interested in what made some people successful while others just plugged along at a lesser level. Why does Tiger Woods continue to outperform other golfers? Why does Katie Couric continue moving up while others get fired? Why does Terry Bradshaw continue to be an anchor in broadcasting long after others have faded? Why, why, why? I was full of questions, and it seemed the only way to get the answers was to go to as many highly successful people as I could, study them, and find out what differences existed between them and their lower-performing peers.

So I did.

We studied everybody we could get access to—and that was a pretty impressive group of people. We studied the top performers on Wall Street, and we studied many of the top performers in industry. We studied many of the world's top athletes from all kinds of sports, and we studied kids who were exceptional in test scores and performance. We studied television personalities, and we studied moms and dads who were doing an outstanding job raising their kids. We studied our nation's top educators, and we studied many of the titans of the manufacturing world. We studied top people in retailing, and we studied top people in the military. We studied everyone we could get information on, and we are still studying people, because we want to continue to refine our understanding of the differences between those who perform at the top and those who don't.

Theories of Success

At the heart of Overcoming Personal Constraints (OPC) is the powerful notion that our strengths do not single-handedly define our success. No matter how formidable our talents, we are held back by *behaviors* that set the limits of our performance or define the reasons for our failure. In other words, *our personal constraints determine our ultimate level of success.* If you can identify those constraints and make a plan to overcome them, then you'll see a dramatic surge in success, productivity, and happiness in all aspects of your life. In short you'll learn who you were born to be.

The Personal Constraint Theory of success challenges two prevailing approaches to self-improvement that frequently did not work for my clients: Personality Theory and Strength Theory. **Personality Theory** asserts that our personalities are essentially fixed in ways that define how we act. A broad field that encompasses several sometimes-conflicting views of "the self," Personality Theory offers little help identifying issues or strategies for improvement. I agree with the underlying idea that our innate characteristics or traits often define who we are, but Personality Theory fails to acknowledge our tremendous capacity for making positive change in our lives and, thus, offers limited use as a tool for growth. Dozens of profiles can describe your personality. Tests such as DiSC, Myers-Briggs, and Taylor-Johnson are interesting to take and helpful in describing your personality, but they are not particularly useful in bringing about behavioral change or directing personal growth.

Another popular school of thought, known as **Strength Theory**, suggests that if we pay attention to the directions in which we move naturally, this can reveal our strengths and show us where to focus our energies. Strength Theory goes something like this: our hardwired personalities resist change, so we should build on our natural abilities instead of concentrating on areas in which we underperform. In other words, to quote the phrase by which this theory has been popularized, we should "play to our strengths." I certainly agree with the basic concept of Strength Theory—why work in an office when you are a gifted musician or stay in a job you hate just because it pays a decent wage? Find your gifts, develop them, and use them for the highest and greatest good.

Strength Theory contributes to success. But it's not enough. If you know your strengths but are trying to get to the next level, playing harder to those strengths won't cause a significant jump in performance. Most people I work with don't need pep talks about being better at what they're already great at or loving themselves as they are. Telling a highly creative person with no self-control to simply celebrate and expand his creativity, for example, would be counterproductive: his or her gifts can never be fully expressed without the focus and discipline that come with self-control.

Neither Personality Theory nor Strength Theory has been greatly useful to my work. The idea that my personality is impervious to change doesn't help me much when I am trying to make my life better. And being told to focus on my strengths doesn't address the behaviors I need to correct in order to move forward.

In contrast, *Overcoming Personal Constraints* is built on the notion that change is more than possible; it is imperative. To live fully we can and must learn how to minimize our behavioral weaknesses while we maximize our strengths. Granted, many obstacles are difficult to overcome, and a single-minded focus on our limitations could be frustrating and even depressing. But to ignore them is even worse.

Personal Constraints Set Your Limits

How do personal constraints determine success?

Simple. They set the limits for where you can ultimately go, no matter how gifted or talented you are. Your personal constraints— your conscious and unconscious limiting behaviors—hold you back and determine your ultimate level of success.

Most of us know at least one person in life who possesses great talents, abilities, gifts, or opportunities yet seems to have done so little with it all. Perhaps you might be looking at your *own* life so far and wondering, *Have I really been living to the fullest of my abilities?* If you're like most people, the answer is, "Probably not."

So what makes some people different? What makes some people rise to the top of their personal or professional spheres? I started looking at people who were categorized as "the best" in their fields. I asked myself: *What makes them the best?* I knew that it was more than their strengths that ultimately made the difference in how people performed.

That is when I came up with the concept of personal constraints. I knew even before all our testing was complete that somehow the answers to my questions lay more in limitations than strengths.

During this data-gathering process, I asked our staff, "Who is the number-one influence in sports?" Immediately one of them said, "Mark McCormack."

From Skeptic to Believer

Mark McCormack was indeed one of the greatest influences in contemporary sports in the last century. He shook hands with Arnold Palmer in 1960 in a deal that changed the endorsement world forever. Prior to that, virtually no one had ever heard of endorsement deals. From that historic moment Mark began building International Management Group (IMG), a global company that represents everyone from Tiger Woods to the pope to Nobel Prize winners.

And I was sitting in Mark McCormack's study, talking to him about how to become better. I had to be either stupid...or onto something.

Mark thought I was stupid. But his wife didn't. She was a well-respected tennis great, having won numerous professional tennis titles in a twenty-three-year career, and she was sitting next to him on the couch. Thank goodness for wives. Betsy said, "If this works, if you can *really* help someone identify the things holding them back—and then do something about them—you can sign me up right here. How do we do it?"

Mark, on the other hand, looked at her enthusiasm with more than a little skepticism and went off to do some work in his office. He was going to be a tough case, and I knew it. An hour later he rejoined us.

I asked him, "Mark, what would you say if I could show you the number-one personal constraint that is holding you back from performing at a much higher level than you are at now?"

He didn't hesitate. "I don't believe you could."

Finally, after some discussion, he decided that he wanted to go through the process himself to explore the concept of personal constraints and how they could impact someone's performance. I joined Mark and Betsy in the den to begin a life-changing growth process.

As we sat discussing Betsy's career, she asked a great question. "If I couldn't get better by practicing more, then what should I have done?" That question brought us to the Flippen Profile, the instrument I had developed and used successfully with so many people.

Betsy was a great tennis player, and she still plays as tough a game as you will ever see. At seventeen, she had been ranked as the world's top junior player. She held five singles titles and twenty-five doubles titles in her amazing career.

When she asked what her personal constraints were, I was really on the spot. I don't know anything about tennis, and I didn't yet know she had played competitively, and I *sure* didn't know that she had won as many tournaments as she had. Yet there was her question: *"What are the personal constraints that are holding me back?"*

I asked Betsy to fill out the Flippen Profile so we could go over the data and see what it identified as her most impacting personal constraints. As we looked over her scores, we turned to the coaching pages that isolated her top personal constraints. The most impacting personal constraints for Betsy were her high-nurturing scales and her low aggression. She did not have the killer instinct required to play at the level she was competing at. In other words her talent and skill had brought her this far, *but her personal constraints would keep her out of the number-one spot.* I am in awe of Betsy's talent and drive. But, ironically, the same love and consideration for others that have made her a wonderful mother and friend turned out to be the constraint that kept her from going on the court and "destroying" the opponent.

When I showed her the data, she leaned back in her chair and sighed. Mark was sitting next to her, and he laughed.

"See? I have been telling you that for years! I was right, wasn't I?"

That created a dilemma for Mark, as he was now seeing that this process was something that he could really agree with. There was another question that he had to answer as well—he had known her for years, and I had known her for less than an hour. *How could I know what I know so quickly?* But the truth was the truth. Betsy was too nurturing and not aggressive enough to be able to win at the level she wanted to play at. This was most apparent when she played against someone she really liked. Her pattern was invariably to lose the first set and then try to come back and win after she had placed herself behind. Creating a handicap is not a good way to play at the top.

"Betsy," I said, "can you imagine what would happen if we could not only *identify* your top personal constraints but create a plan so you could start immediately to *overcome* them?"

Well, she could, and she did—and so did Mark.

Throwing Out the Weights

A few years ago I took my boys Matthew and Micah on our annual guys' outing: a grueling, six-day, backpacking trip in the mountains of Colorado.

The morning after we arrived in Beaver Creek, we went to the ski area where we would begin our hike. We put on our packs and began to head toward the lift that would take us up to our starting point. As we rounded the corner of a large building at the base of the mountain, the entire plain ahead of us literally exploded with color. We could hardly believe our eyes!

We had no idea we had just walked into the biggest ballooning event in the country. Mesmerized by the scene of balloonists preparing for flight, we watched as hot-air balloons of every color in the rainbow swelled with air and began to fill the sky. Pilots and crews scurried about. Blasts from tiny furnaces punctuated the morning bustle, and inflated balloons strained to lift their passengers to the heavens, held fast as they waited for the ropes to be removed.

One balloon caught my eye. Most people were running away from it because it had become dangerous—the furnace had stopped firing hot air into the balloon before it had fully inflated. Half filled and tethered by a long rope, it was slowly arcing its way in a circle, knocking over everything in its path like an enormous plush bowling ball. A crew member was frantically struggling to untie a rope that wouldn't budge while the balloon wreaked havoc in slow motion. As we watched from a distance, the balloon continued "butt bumping" along the field, as it pulled and lurched against the restraints. I looked at Matthew and Micah and said, "Boys, I know just what that feels like."

"What do you mean, Dad?" Matthew asked.

"I know what it's like—wanting to get off the ground, but tied to something, and trying desperately to break free." I went on to explain that I could remember various times that unseen "ropes" kept me tied down when I wanted to soar. Despite my mistakes and failures, I knew I was meant for more. *Cut me loose and let me go—I WANT TO FLY!*

Later, as we watched the balloons rise toward the heavens from a mountaintop where we were sitting, I reflected further on the striking similarities we share with them. I realized that we are *all* riding in a hot-air balloon. And whether we recognize it or not, we are all in a race. Some of us are still tied to the ground, looking for a way to get loose so we can take flight. Then there are those who are lifting off but not gaining any altitude because they are carrying too much weight. The ropes and weights hold them down as they try to move up and out.

As we begin our ascent, we notice that some balloons are immediately soaring upward, while others are hovering along the surface, barely clearing the ground. Then someone runs up and yells at one of those struggling to get off the ground, "It's the weights! *Throw out the weights!*"

After a moment the person in the gondola gets it. *It's the weights that are holding me down!* They begin to throw the weights overboard as fast as they can, and sure enough, the balloon begins to rise.

The journey you are about to take is all about you: your balloon, your weights, your ropes, the things that hold you down. You can choose to live life as you always have, *or* you can choose to identify and overcome what has held you back. *You can fly*—and the air, the scenery, and life itself will be so much more exhilarating as you discover how to overcome the personal constraints that have been holding you down.

Let's find the weights in your life...and throw them overboard.

3 The Five Laws of Personal Constraints

More than three decades separated the work I had done with Janice and Tony from the time I spent with Peter and Daniel.

During those years my company has had the privilege of working with some of the most outstanding leaders of business, sports, and education of our time. The information we gathered told the same story: in every field talented and capable people were short-circuiting their own success. But they were also finding that they could fulfill their potential once they could identify and overcome the constraints that were holding them back. Drawing on these experiences and insights, we created a complete system for identifying the specific factors that limit our performance. They could then develop a personalized plan for growing through them.

At the heart of this system is a set of simple principles that describe the impact of personal constraints in your life. I call them the Five Laws of Personal Constraints. Used together these laws provide a solid foundation for the personal-growth program presented in the chapters that follow.

Law One: *We All Have Personal Constraints*

We all know of public figures who make the headlines daily as they fall prey to rage, greed, and moral failures. But we also know of constraints being played out on a smaller scale—parents who are too critical of their children, the boss who is too defensive to hear feedback. Having constraints is part of being human. I have them. Everybody I know has them. And you have them, too. As we've seen, some constraints are more damaging than others. There's no point focusing on minor inconveniences when a potential train wreck is waiting somewhere ahead.

As I was developing the OPC process, I found that personal constraints fell into three basic groups:

1. *InconsequentialConstraints:* This group doesn't make a great difference on a daily basis unless they hinder a specific role or job. For example, a lack of fashion sense, being short or tall, or being left-handed generally have minimal impact on success.

2. *"Hire-able" Constraints:* These are constraints that you can hire someone else to do for you. They could be critical but are not if the solutions are provided by others. "Hire-able" constraints include things like messiness (hire a housekeeper), disorganization (hire a secretary or assistant), and poor grammar (use a spell-check program or hire an editor).

3. *OwnedConstraints:* This category will impact your personal and professional life most profoundly. One thing I keep trying to do is hire someone to do my gym workout for me—but it never seems to work. These constraints include behaviors such as low self-confidence and self-control and other character issues (for example, lack of trustworthiness) that you alone can change. Addressing this group will give you the greatest gains.

The focus of all that we will be discussing in this book is on those behaviors in the third category. I have little interest in spending a lot of time working on constraints that are inconsequential or negligible. Those things that I can hire others to do certainly have importance, but they will always be secondary to those critical constraints that only I can address and correct.

After we have reviewed our goals, roles, and relationships, we are in a better position to see which constraints we can ignore, hire out, or own. Knowing the difference is key to identifying the constraints that are impacting our success the most. Only then can we expect to start getting the results we want.

Law Two: *You Can't Rise Above Constraints That You Don't or Won't Address*

There is an old story about how hunters catch monkeys in Africa. They hollow out a coconut, making sure the hole is just large enough for a monkey's hand, then place a small orange or banana inside and chain the coconut to a tree. The scent attracts the monkey, who sticks his hand into the coconut but soon discovers the hole is not big enough for him to remove both his hand *and* the prize. To get his hand out, he must drop what he's holding. But he won't. He is so intent on getting his treat that he will not even drop it to escape as the hunter easily captures him.

Do you see the picture?

Many of us are held captive by the constraints we continue to clutch tenaciously—including unresolved issues from our past—because we can't or won't address them. Like the monkey we are paralyzed and stuck between two worlds, not realizing we are choosing denial at the expense of freedom.

Think of young Tony landing in prison or Daniel's unwillingness to examine himself. The problems that they didn't deal with kept them stuck and unable to grow in those areas. In Daniel's case success in other parts of his life may have lulled him into thinking that he didn't need to work on his shortcomings; Tony, having gone to prison, on the other hand, probably never believed he could change in positive ways.

Both positions are sadly misleading: overcoming our constraints is both possible and necessary if we desire to live life to its fullest. Coming to terms with this simple fact will help us let go of the old to embrace the new.

Law Three: *Our Personal Constraints Play Themselves Out in Every Area of Our Lives*

There's a reason why I encouraged Peter to get specific feedback from both his colleagues and his wife: issues that show up at the office are likely to follow us home. You may have heard the phrase, "Wherever you go, there you are." This is true for our constraints, as well; *they* go wherever *we* go. The point of recognizing this is not to condemn ourselves and our limitations but to more fully understand their impact. If you are difficult at work, odds are good that you are just as difficult at home.

Personal constraints come in many forms. Although most are behavioral, now and then there will be a physical or intellectual constraint so distracting that it works against everything else you may be doing to get ahead in life. Yet as obvious as it may be, everyone pretends not to see it, thinking they are doing a kindness, when in fact, they are simply hurting the other person by not addressing it.

Take Richard's situation, for example.

We had just finished meeting with the senior executives of a company with whom we were working. Before I left I wanted to debrief with them. I had a question for one of the two men sitting at the table with me.

"Tell me about Richard," I said. "He seems like a bright guy with a lot of potential."

The CEO quickly responded, "He's very smart, and he has a great work ethic."

My next question surprised them. "Well, tell me about the knot on his head. Do you know anything about it?"

They looked at each other. It seemed that neither of them wanted to acknowledge what was—to me—Richard's most defining physical characteristic: a large, protruding bump on one side of his forehead. One of them finally answered. "When he was hired he had that knot on his head, but it's gotten bigger since then. At first it wasn't a problem because his job and area of responsibility were limited. But these days he's in meetings with customers all day, and he represents the company at many functions. We've never talked to him about it— how would we even bring it up?"

"I'll talk to him and see what the problem is," I said. They both looked shocked that I wanted to attempt a discussion about it. I scheduled our next visit and asked that I also be allowed to meet with a few of their people privately, including Richard, so that I could go over their personal-constraint data with them.

I didn't understand why no one had talked to him about it earlier, but then again, I'm a shrink. My desire is to address *everything* that appears to be affecting someone's well-being and chances for success in life. Although some things are unchangeable in life, I believe that category is much smaller than we think. In this case I wanted to know more. Although it was a delicate issue, its ramifications were not. How do you ignore a knot on a man's forehead the size of a golf ball? It was just about dead center over his right eye.

When I returned, Richard and I sat down in his office, and after we had visited for a few minutes, I brought it up.

"Richard, tell me about the knot on your head, will you?"

He looked at me the same way his two bosses had and said, "Does it bother you?"

"No, not at all," I replied. "But it's probably getting in the way of where you are going professionally, and *that* bothers me. I'd like to know if there's some way to help."

Then he told me the story: "Flip, when I was in high school, I was a tough ball player, but I was only five feet nine inches and that didn't cut it, so I did steroids. I had some knots come up on my arms and one on my back within six months, and then this one started growing within a year. At the time I thought it was worth it to compete against the big guys, but now I have to live with the fallout of the choices I made back then."

I asked, "Have you ever had anyone look at it to see if it could be removed?" He shook his head thoughtfully.

"What do you think your wife would say if we asked her about it?"

He looked at me and chuckled. "Do you know any woman who wants to be married to a knot-head?" I appreciated his candor and sense of humor about the whole thing, and we agreed that his knot might not have to be the first thing people noticed about him. He would go to his doctor to see what could be done about it.

Richard got the appointment, and after examination, the doctor encouraged him to have it removed immediately because the mass had begun to attach itself to his skull. His insurance paid for most of it, and his boss paid the deductible. With his lump removed and his life most likely lengthened, Richard's story had a happy ending.

But the questions are worth examining: *Is it good for a man to go through life with a knot on his head that no one ever mentions? Should people let friends, family members, and coworkers go from day to day with something that is obviously hindering their performance, appearance, and/or success without looking for a way to help them if at all possible? Is risking a moment or two of embarrassment worth getting rid of—once and for all—the elephant in the room?* Richard's knot went with him everywhere and likely was the focus of more than one private joke or conversation.

Of course this is not a typical situation, and as a psychotherapist, I do have the benefit of people understanding I am there to help them. In matters that require extra sensitivity, generally the privilege of speaking about personal or difficult subjects must be earned through relationship and trust. And you might first check your motives and make sure you are doing it because you want what is best for *the other person,* not because it bothers *you.*

Further, many of us probably don't realize some personal constraints are just as visible to others as a "knot on our head"—constraints that people won't mention yet are distracting them from our greatest attributes. We need to look honestly at the impact every constraint has on us and on those around us—loved ones, family members, employees—all of whom deserve the best we can give them. There is a good chance that we might find something we need to improve. We might even discover it isn't as difficult as we thought and that the rewards far outweigh our initial fears.

Law Four: *Personal Constraints Are Role Specific*

I was born with dyscalcula, a math learning disability. Can you imagine what would happen if I were an accountant? My struggle with numbers would not make me a good hire for that job. I'd probably plunge the company into bankruptcy and land the entire management team in prison. While behaviors tend to leak into every compartment of life, paradoxically, they become constraints only when they get in the way of attaining specific goals.

The impact of our constraints can vary depending on what role or context we are in. Behavior that restricts us in one area might be an asset in another. A junior-high-school teacher, for example, will have a lot more trouble with a high level of aggression when he's teaching math class than when he's coaching football after school, although his aggression will need to be managed in every area of life. Being methodically analytical probably helps a physician in private practice but can be a hindrance for someone in a fast-moving sales or marketing position and an irritation in relationships, where majoring in minor issues can wear thin pretty fast.

Having low aggression doesn't work for a race-car driver, and having low self-confidence doesn't work for a heart surgeon. I don't want to have a teacher who is low nurturing, nor do I want to have an accountant who thrives on creativity. Our personal constraints are role specific—pure and simple.

To understand our constraints fully, we must consider them in terms of the various roles we play in life. We need to evaluate each constraint in context and determine whether it is keeping us from performing our best in a given position or situation.

Law Five: *Those with the Fewest Constraints...WIN*

Here we get to the heart of OPC: the reward for the removal of our constraints. We have been able to prove year after year, with thousands of success stories, *that people who actively choose to identify and remove their personal constraints will fare better than those who do not.* It boils down to physics: the lighter the load you carry, the farther you can go. This final law provides hope: you can do something about your current situation that will also have an impact on your future.

But it gets slightly tricky here, so follow me. I am not saying that people *with the lowest number of constraints* win, but rather, those who *learn to minimize or eradicate significant constraints* win. A significant constraint is one that gets in the way on a regular basis and causes damage to relationships and your ability to produce great work. Those with the fewest significant constraints will outperform those with more significant constraints. This concept needs closer examination because the thoughts behind it are so important.

It is true that many people are simply born with fewer personal constraints than others. For example, Vern Hazard, one of my staff members, has been an international model and traveled all over the world. Vern is handsome, athletic, and an English scholar, as well. Most of us don't come with the gifts and talents that he naturally possesses. But being born with fewer personal limitations and constraints is *not* the same as personal growth. Personal growth refers to working on everything in your life that stops you from living to your full potential.

One of my good friends, Mark Stiles, uses a baseball analogy that I find most appropriate for this picture. He says, "There are guys who were born on third base but are convinced they hit a triple." Being born with advantage, family influence, talents, gifts, and abilities is not the same as personal growth, nor should we confuse someone who comes loaded with these attributes with someone who has learned how to use his gifts in valuable ways. Vern works hard to be the best at everything he does. Yes, he's gifted, but it's his passion and drive that set him apart.

Ultimately this book is about *winning*. By winning I don't mean that you compete in races or make the most money. I mean that you become your personal best. That you win at being *you*—the best you there is.

4 Overview: The Top 10 Killer Constraints

We all have constraints that are potentially hurtful and sometimes dangerous. What about a parent who isn't nurturing enough to his or her children? Or a parent who is too nurturing and continues to enable inappropriate behavior by not setting adequate boundaries? What about a boss or a spouse who is defensive and not open to feedback? It is easy to minimize the threat that our constraints pose, but even constraints that appear to be harmless sometimes play themselves out on a larger scale. How do we find out what those constraints are? What can we do about them?

I have called these things that hinder our performance personal constraints because that is how they function. They constrain us from moving forward, from rising higher, and from seeing the world from a fresh perspective.

The truth is that *we all have constraints*. And we all have more than one, or two, or three. The key is to identify and change those constraints that have the biggest impact on your life. Remember the story I told about the hot-air balloon? You can throw out either the one-pound weights or the twenty-pound weights. I can assure you that throwing out the twenty-pound weights will give you the greatest lift. If we want to remove the weights, or personal constraints, that hold us back, we must identify and take steps to break the constraints that have the greatest impact on our lives.

In my work as a psychotherapist, I have two important tasks I must accomplish for every patient: first, I must make a diagnosis and second, I must prescribe the proper treatment. The diagnosis of any situation is critical. If the diagnosis is wrong, then it is difficult—if not impossible—to prescribe the correct treatment.

In life we frequently fail to make the connection between the pain or frustration we may be experiencing in a given situation and the true source of that pain, which is often a hidden behavior or set of behaviors.

I have a colleague who has diagnosed many of his patients as having bipolar disorder. He was great at treating bipolar issues, and after a while, it seemed that every patient he saw had bipolar disorder. But many of the diagnoses were wrong. At that point it didn't matter how good he was at treating bipolar disorder—the diagnosis was wrong, so the treatment was useless at best and damaging at worst. Diagnosis is everything when it comes to assessing a problem. *Wrong diagnosis leads to wrong treatment.*

So how do we identify the problem correctly and begin the process of change?

Clarity of Focus

One Saturday morning as I was putting on my work clothes and preparing to take my horse, Mikey, to check on things at the ranch, Susan asked if I would sit and talk with her for a moment. I really didn't like the thought of losing time, but I could see that she had something on her mind, and I adore her, so what could I say? As we talked Susan began to share with me that I really do work too much. She felt that I needed to do something to relax and take my mind off business and work. I was resistant at first because I enjoy the things I do, but I also knew she was making a good point.

Then she shocked me.

"Why don't you start playing golf?"

That was the last thing I expected her to say, and I sat there with a seriously dumb look on my face. "Honey, I haven't played golf since I was a kid. Where would I begin, and why would I do it in the first place?" She had already thought of those questions before she brought up the subject. She answered each of my concerns, then closed the deal.

"The next time you're in Florida, why don't you take a lesson from one of the pros and see if it's something you would enjoy?" she suggested. I thought about it and agreed that I would.

Within a few months I found myself standing on a driving range in Florida with a well-known coach. This pro had worked with some top golfers and great athletes...and he was giving me a look that suggested I was neither! After they filmed my swing (I'm sure they recorded it for others' entertainment), we went through the next (and most humbling) part of the lesson. He started telling me all the things that were wrong with my swing: I needed to change my grip on the club, I should bend my knees more, and I needed to turn my hips more on the follow-through part of my swing. I wasn't following the same arc with each swing—this had to be fixed, or I would never be consistent. Then came the discussion about my wrists and how "wristy" (whatever that is) I was, which was, of course, messing up my arc even when I had it right because I was letting my wrists act "independently," something they apparently weren't supposed to be doing.

There were also comments about keeping my head still while swinging and, at the same time, keeping my back straight. With each new instruction I was forgetting the other things I was supposed to do. I was so confused at the end of the lesson that I didn't know what was going on. Too much stuff. I felt like Charlie Brown on the football field, paralyzed and unable to do anything.

I was glad to get on the plane and fly home. A few months later I was taking another golf lesson, but this time it was from Jeff Hunter, the head professional at Miramont Country Club in Bryan, Texas. Jeff is a great teacher. As we stood on the range, he watched for a while as I hit a few balls.

"You need to swing through your strokes more," he said, demonstrating his point as he let the club come all the way around so that he finished in a picture-perfect pose at the end of the swing. I tried a few practice swings myself, experiencing how different this slight adjustment felt. After a minute or two, I was surprised to see Jeff turn his back to me and start walking back to the clubhouse.

"*Whoa*...wait a minute! Where are you going?" I called to him.

"That's all you need for now," he replied. "Work on that, and we'll talk when you get that down."

That was it—that was all I had to do. I was impressed. An hour later he was back. As he walked up he commented, "You need to keep working on that. There's more, but that is the one thing that will give you the most gain for now. Just keep practicing that, and we'll talk in a few weeks." And off he went.

One thing. Just do this, and we'll talk later after you have it down. Those words were sweet to my ears because he had found the starting point for me. This was something that I could really work on and see improvement. There weren't ten things that I had to think about— there was one thing. *Swing through with the club and stand there.* I have to admit I thought I looked pretty good standing there with that picture-perfect finish. Not that I had any idea where the ball was going, but I sure looked good.

Still scoring well up in the nineties, I was ready for my next lesson. It was even better. His next point was that I needed to add to my "great finish," making good contact with the ball. And off he went again.

With each succeeding lesson he added one more point. Of course there were more comments than I am including here, but the point was always the same: "Flip, you can't fix it all at once. There is only so much you can work on at one time. You need to know what changes will actually give you the greatest gains. That's what you want to work on—the thing that is holding you back the most." What a smart way to go. I'm still not where I want to be as a golfer, but I am doing a lot better and am always ready for the next lesson and game.

There is another thought I want to throw in at this point. Would you say the biggest reason for my inability to score in the eighties was my clubs or my lack of experience? Of course it was my lack of experience. But how many golfers do you know who are constantly changing clubs only to find that they still don't shoot any better? If you are changing things that don't make any difference at the expense of ignoring the ones that do, you are wasting your money and your time, not to mention the frustration you will feel when all your efforts fail to produce greater gains.

Jeff showed me how to focus on a single thing—one step at a time—in my quest to improve my golf game. There is one thing and one place to start for every challenge we meet.

OPC is no different. First, you identify your biggest constraint—the one thing that will give you the highest payoff—and you go to work to change that. After you have broken through that one, then you go to work on the next most significant constraint. This is the process, and it focuses on the one thing that you need to be doing at that particular time.

Keep in mind that this *is* a process. If you are truly growing, then it is a never-ending process. You will work through the first constraint and then go on to identify the next one. With each additional step you will find that your life is truly improving and that you are performing at a higher level.

It doesn't matter if your most crucial personal constraint is that you talk too much or don't talk enough. It isn't important if your greatest constraint is that you are lazy, or shy, or that you have low self-control, or that you spend so much time organizing your life that you never live it. What *is* important is that you don't have the same level of personal constraints next year that you have this year. That is growth.

The goal for anyone seeking to improve his or her performance is to remove the top constraints in their makeup. To do this you must "diagnose" or identify your constraints, then "fill the prescription" and execute a plan to break or overcome your constraints.

Identify Your Constraints

The most useful diagnosis is one that identifies something that can be changed. So the first step in this process is getting an accurate assessment of the top one or two constraints that are affecting your life the most. Our constraints can include any behavior, attribute, or psychological condition that prevents us from performing at our highest level.

This framework inevitably includes some constraints that can't be changed, such as physical limitations; no matter how much you might want to play basketball, for example, you can't make yourself taller. The focus of Overcoming Personal Constraints (OPC) is on our *behavior,* because our actions are within the range of what we are able to control. If we can address our limiting behaviors, we can effect significant change in our lives. This fact leads us to the question at the center of personal growth: *what behaviors do I need to change and how can I change them?*

Feedback Is Critical

Unfortunately we are often the worst judges of our own situations. Our constraints may have developed because we just don't see them, or they may directly impede our ability to recognize them. Either way my years as a psychotherapist have convinced me that self-assessment is not something that can be done effectively in isolation. I've asked lots of people over the years to name their top areas needing improvements, and very few have any sort of accurate response.

The fact of the matter is that self-assessment is an oxymoron. You can't get a self-help book and sit alone and read it and think you have accurately assessed yourself *by* yourself. Although it is a good start, your own assessment is only part of the equation. If I went through life without feedback, I might think that I have great hair (even as it gets thinner every year) and have what it takes to be a world-class jockey (not likely at six feet three inches). The problem is that reality does not always bear out our favorite illusions about ourselves, and I want to live in reality (at least for the most part, I do). I can't fully self-assess by myself, so I must get others' input to have a more complete picture. Although this book offers all the tools you'll need to put together a plan for success in overcoming your personal constraints, it is the people around you who hold many of the keys to effective diagnosis.

Recently I was packing to go out of town, and two of the boys were sitting on the ledge of the tub in our bathroom. They were giving me a hard time about what I was wearing, and I turned and looked in the mirror, commenting that I was sure thankful that I had a full head of hair and looked as good as I did (they had really been harassing me). Of course one of them couldn't resist.

"Well, Pop, you need to slip around back and take another look!" They both laughed until I ran them out.

Next time I'll get ready by myself.

But it certainly illustrated a basic problem with mankind. We are social animals, and we need help assessing our strengths and weaknesses. Hopefully some of the people who will help you self-assess (more on this later) will be kinder to you than those two were to me. Mind you, I did get over it.

When Motivation Meets Science

Years ago my company began a long and rigorous development process to identify personal constraints. We gathered and compared behavioral and attitudinal data from top performers in a variety of fields, including corporate executives, schoolteachers, professional athletes, stay-at-home moms, administrative assistants, construction workers, midlevel managers, salespeople, doctors, and ranch managers.

I wanted to know which traits they consistently had in common, but I also wanted to know what makes these people different from others who seem to perpetually struggle. So I took this a step further, gathering data on low performers as well.

As we analyzed the information, we were struck by the findings. Even across occupations, the top achievers had consistent patterns in common that distinguished them from low achievers. Combining this information with my decades of case studies and counseling notes, we devised a truly unique and statistically valid process.

I well remember the first time we compared data for high performers against data for low performers. The statistical differences confirmed all our projections and validated our process of measuring and quantifying behavioral attributes that were associated with both success and the lack of it.

Through all of this we have found ten critical constraints that—either alone or in combinations with other constraints—repeatedly did the most damage to personal growth, relationships, and careers.

We have named them the Top 10 Killer Constraints and will highlight them with stories and illustrations so you can recognize these behaviors in yourself and others. This process is designed to give you an effective "diagnosis and prescription"—complete with steps to begin the process of breaking each constraint.

As you read the chapters and complete the corresponding assessments, remember that each assessment is just part of the identification process. You may find that you have many symptoms from one constraint, a few from several constraints, or several symptoms from a few. You may even find that you have only two or three symptoms from one personal constraint, but if these symptoms are found frequently at the "scene of the crime" in work and relationship troubles, then each one needs to be treated seriously if you truly desire to move forward in life. To be clear, there are a few people who may not have a dangerous level of any of the constraints, but shades of certain constraints can surface, especially during times of stress. Additionally there is a section at the end of each personal-constraint chapter to help you deal effectively with that constraint when you encounter it in those around you. We all influence and impact each other for better or worse, and understanding *why* we do *what* we do is a great start to helping others turn their lives around.

To give you a snapshot of the nature of these constraints, we have personified each of them for you:

- Bulletproof (Overconfident)
- Ostriches (Low Self-Confidence)
- Marshmallows (Overly Nurturing)
- Critics (Too Demanding, Nitpicky, or Harsh)
- Icebergs (Low Nurturing)
- Flatliners (Low Passion, Vision, or Drive)
- Bulldozers (Overly Dominant)
- Turtles (Resistant to Change)
- Volcanoes (Aggressive, Angry)
- Quick Draw (Low Self-Control, Impulsive)

PART
II

Identifying
Personal
Constraints

What's Your Personal Constraint?

In the chapters that follow, you'll learn about the Top 10 Killer Constraints that most of us are faced with (either in ourselves or in the people around us). But before we discuss each constraint in more detail, here's a quick assessment to help you start thinking about which constraints are holding you back . . . and what areas you might need to do the most work on.

- Is it hard for you to admit fault?
- Are you opinionated?
- Is your first reaction to feedback to think about why it isn't accurate?

If so, you might be ***Bulletproof***.

- Do you wish you were more confident?
- Is it important what other people think of you?
- Do you have a hard time moving on from your mistakes?

If so, you might be an ***Ostrich***.

- Do you ever struggle with saying no?
- Is it difficult for you to say what you really think?
- Do you frequently find yourself being overcommitted and worn out?

If so, you might be a ***Marshmallow***.

- Do you have high expectations of yourself and others?
- Are you usually skeptical of ideas and opinions?
- Do you remember the mistakes other people make?

If so, you might be a ***Critic***.

- Has anyone said you are hard to read?
- Do you ever wonder why other people have closer relationships than you do?
- Do you struggle expressing affection and emotion?

If so, you might be an ***Iceberg***.

- Do you struggle to motivate yourself?
- Do you procrastinate frequently?
- Do people misinterpret your laid-back tendencies?

If so, you might be a *Flatliner*.

- Is being in control important to you?
- Do your strong opinions cause others to perceive you as not listening?
- Do you finish other people's sentences?

If so, you might be a *Bulldozer*.

- Do change and uncertainty make you nervous?
- Is it hard for you to switch directions easily?
- Do you prefer tried-and-true approaches?

If so, you might be a *Turtle*.

- In disagreements, do you tend to get the last word in?
- Do your emotions escalate when you feel challenged?
- Do you get frustrated with people frequently?

If so, you might be a *Volcano*.

- Do you thrive on spontaneity?
- Do you make quick decisions?
- Do you get bored easily?

If so, you might be a *Quick Draw*.

5 *Killer Constraint #1:* Bulletproof (Overconfident)

In psychology there is a concept that refers to those who have ego-related delusions of grandeur. It is called a Napoleonic complex. And there is a reason the very name, Napoléon, represents the constraint of overconfidence.

On the night of June 23, 1812, Napoléon led his troops across the Niemen River to begin his invasion of Russia. He was set on defeating two of Russia's armies and adding Russia to his list of conquered nations. He had almost 500,000 troops of the entire French Grande Armée of 600,000 in his command for this campaign.

The march to Moscow was a long and arduous one. In the less than five months it took to travel from Paris to Moscow, he lost more than 380,000 men. The lack of supplies, the devastation of disease and dysentery, the loss of thousands of horses and carriages, as well as the despondency of trying to engage an enemy that was strategically withdrawing from the conflict while laying waste to everything, were overwhelming. Napoléon made outrageous requests of his troops all along the way. By the time he reached Moscow on September 14, he had only 100,000 men left.

Yet, in utter denial of the bitter and humiliating defeat, the megalomaniacal Napoléon reported the account of the battle at Smolensk in such a way that one would think he was part of a completely different war: "I was maneuvering in a country which was as well disposed towards me as France itself; the population and authorities were on my side; I was able to obtain men, horses, provisions; and Smolensk is a fortified town" (1812, *Memoirs of Napoleon*).

This was not even close to the truth. He was not welcomed, nor was he successful in obtaining horses or provisions. In fact he had lost about 7,000 men in taking Smolensk. Napoléon could not see past his own ego. His self-confidence was not a guiding light that gave him assurance as he moved forward; it was a blinding light that obscured reality.

Arriving in Moscow was supposed to be a glorious victory, but it was a hollow one at best. The Russians themselves had emptied and torched Moscow rather than allowing Napoléon to have it. With less than a quarter of his men alive, nothing but a burned city as a prize, and fears of losing control back in France, Napoléon had no choice but to return to Paris. A brutal Russian winter had begun, and his army was dogged the entire trip by the Russians and Cossacks as the pitiful Grande Armée was forced to use the same scorched route home, with no shelter, food, or supplies.

Napoléon had begun with almost 500,000 soldiers but returned to Paris with fewer than 10,000 men. In less than one year, he had lost almost a half million soldiers.

Yet Napoléon declared his campaign a victory!

He entered Paris with all the pomp and circumstance of a victorious leader returning from a military sweep. Confident in his reality he declared his victory over the Russians and celebrated his defeat of Moscow.

And herein lies the crucial point. Napoléon was confident in his reality. Not reality, but *his* reality.

Self-confidence is generally a good thing. In proper balance it is a great thing. But overconfidence is perhaps one of the most lethal personal constraints of the Top 10 Killer Constraints. I have watched people bet their entire life's savings on a hunch. Even after losing all they owned, they *still* believed they were right. Because, in their own eyes, they were Bulletproof.

If it was only their future or their life they were risking, it might not be so bad for a person to bet all they have on something they believe in.

But that's not how it works.

People with this personal constraint stake everything they have on the idea that they're right. Unfortunately that "everything" usually involves other people's lives and futures, as well.

Napoléon didn't bet *his* future on his Russian campaign. He bet *other* people's futures—their lives—on his goals. A half million men and their families lost *everything* on his failed Russian gamble. The reason for the invasion in the first place was Napoléon's belief that he did not have to accept a treaty and could, in fact, have it all with a war conquest. Unfortunately Napoléon's Russian victory turned out to be Russian roulette, except—unknown to him—every chamber was loaded. Afterward, his ego refused to allow him to admit the catastrophe he had created.

Leadership has special demands and responsibilities placed upon it. Those in positions of leadership must always weigh gains against losses and ultimately be willing to pay the price that they expect others to pay. For example, I do not have the right as a business owner to ask my staff to support something I want to undertake if I am unwilling to match any sacrifices that they must make in order for it to happen.

Napoléon's overconfidence kept him from seeing the reality of what he was doing. How do you walk past thousands of dead men, thousands of dead horses, and thousands of men dying of typhus and starvation day after day yet not see that something is terribly wrong? It's easy—if you are blind. Overconfidence is a deadly, blinding force.

We see it in public servants, like the politician who stands before the people and denies the truth, believing that he is above the law and that the end justifies the means. We see it in kids who can't accept the reality that someone else won the competition they were sure was theirs. We see it in men and women who risk all they have only to fail, yet never see that the failure was directly tied to their inability to accurately assess a situation due to their extreme self-confidence.

One of the greatest indicators of whether overconfidence is a constraint is a person's ability to openly listen to others' input. Once you quit listening to others, the only voice you have left is your own. That can be a very lonely and deceptive voice, especially if you always think you're right. Napoléon didn't listen. He didn't have to—he was Bulletproof. Except that he wasn't.

After a career decline that began with his doomed Russian invasion, Napoléon was exiled twice, and he died on the island of St. Helena after a lengthy illness amid rumors of arsenic poisoning.

Too Much *Dot-com*-fidence

Like Lucy from the *Peanuts* comic strip, those who have extremely high self-confidence often display a forceful, take-charge type of personality. We see this behavior in many of today's most exciting careers and activities, as well as more mainstream positions such as sales and marketing executives. Extremely self-confident people often have magnetic personalities, and they always seem to have an answer for everything. Many entrepreneurs struggle with this constraint. In one sense they must have high self-confidence in order to take a risk to start something that others can't, or won't, do. But if high self-confidence is not balanced by other traits, such as self-control and/or humility, it will eventually cause more harm than good.

During the dot-com days of the late nineties, I remember sitting in Dallas with some investors as they reviewed some opportunities being presented to them. During one of the meetings, I sat across from the former president of a dot-com startup as he presented his idea about a hot, new venture. He had just sold his stock in his first startup, and he made sure we knew that he had made a killing in the market. Clearly he expected to be trusted with venture capital to do the deal he was currently presenting due to his hot streak. His history was dotted with many short-term ventures. The most striking thing about him was his flamboyant and showy style. From his continual name-dropping to the designer label he was careful to display as he folded his coat inside out on the chair next to him, he started more than a few red flags waving in the wind.

In the group discussion that followed, I raised a question about the basic business plan that seemed to be missing from the presentation. My doubts were quickly discounted by most of the other attendees. "You were probably the last guy on your block to replace your rotary dial phone with a touch-tone model!" joked the dot-com dynamo.

They plowed ahead with discussions focusing on how much money they would make and when they would go "public" with their ideas. The numbers were based on the idea that people would flock to their site to see the latest news or opportunity and then they would sell advertising to those who came to their site; that was how they would ultimately make money. There was no marketing research given to support the high dollar figures or any of the claims being made that day. I continued to ask basic questions about the lack of a business plan and the business leader's pattern of moving constantly from one idea to the next without staying around long enough to actually finish any of them.

All of the presenter's ideas were wrapped up in a charismatic style that seemed big on chance and short on content, yet the appeal of the dot-com opportunities of those days resulted in my questions (and those of one other colleague) being quickly dismissed. In the final analysis several of the people in the room bought into the concept because of the presenter's extremely high self-confidence. He sold his idea so well they were sure he had to succeed.

But he didn't.

The business venture cost the investors more than $5 million before the company was ultimately shut down.

And our well-dressed presenter? He got paid an annual salary of $250,000 for leading a charge that ultimately failed. And, true to form, he left the company before it went under because he had another, hotter, newer idea he felt he needed to offer to another group of investors.

Although he got the deal on little more than his persuasive style, it cost him credibility and a future with the group that chose to invest with him. Because venture capital investors tend to know each other, you can be sure that at some point his ways will catch up with him. The "dealer" will eventually have to deal with himself.

Of course they say that hindsight is always twenty-twenty, and it is easy to see problems looking back, but I knew at the time that the dot-com parade would be a washout.

How?

It's not that I was so smart—it was all in the data. After profiling many of the dot-com business leaders, we mapped almost identical behavioral traits—all led by off-the-charts self-confidence.

Are You Bulletproof?

Check any of the following symptoms that occur and add up the total.

- ☐ I am a key contributor to the success and accomplishments of the teams I work on.
- ☐ You will rarely find people who can perform at my level.
- ☐ When I have a new idea, I press forward and don't ask for feedback from others about the best way to proceed.
- ☐ I am not really concerned with how other people view me or how they feel about me.
- ☐ Some people think I'm arrogant at times, but I'm just telling it like it is.
- ☐ I really believe in my hunches, even when the facts don't bear me out.
- ☐ It's not unusual for people to tell me that they don't feel like I'm listening.
- ☐ When it comes to admitting fault, I may accept some blame, but I focus on the other person's failings.

☐ When I have a conflict with someone, I rarely stop to objectively reflect or to ask someone else exactly how I contributed to the conflict.

☐ I can sometimes sound condescending when expressing my opinions.

Bulletproof Tendencies?

Mark your total below.

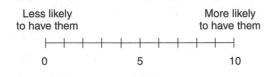

So I'm Bulletproof—Help Me!

I'm in an interesting position—trying to communicate to the strongest personalities that they might need to make some adjustments. Sort of like selling ice to an Eskimo!

A friend of mine was taking the Flippen Profile recently and got to the word "stubborn." He didn't know whether it really applied to him, so he asked his wife, "Honey, am I stubborn?" After a few seconds of silence, the answer was clear. "What?" he clarified. "I'm not stubborn. If someone presents a differing opinion and he or she provides an argument that makes sense to me, I can easily adapt my thinking. That's not stubborn." After a few more seconds of silence, the answer was again clear. A lot of level-headed people frequently appear stubborn, and perception is reality. So a key theme I'd like you to look into is teachability. Do you think you are teachable? Do others think you are—or do they feel like ice peddlers in Alaska?

In some ways this can be one of the most crippling constraints because people will stop giving feedback if it isn't wanted. And watch for asking too many clarification questions the next time you are getting feedback—that's a killer, too. Even if some of the feedback was confusing, a simple "thank you" is sufficient for the moment; then decide later if clarification is appropriate.

Another key theme is "dragging" people versus bringing them alongside. I don't know very many people who like or will even put up with being dragged, so be careful of your approach. I've noticed that some people talk so loud that no one can hear them. This is unfortunate, because they may have great insight, but people tune them out. Make sure you are on the right wavelength for people to hear your opinions.

Even Eskimos need some ice every once in a while!

Specific TrAction Steps

Here are some sample action steps you can take to start getting traction—today! Once you read all of the constraint chapters, if this is determined to be one of your killer constraints, then steps like these will be part of your TrAction Plan (to be built in chapter 15).

• I will start asking for feedback from someone with a strong personality. I will determine a couple of questions that are targeted to areas I am working on (for example, "Have I appeared stubborn recently?" or "Have I been tending to people enough recently?"), and I will have someone grade me on a one-to-ten scale each week. If I receive a score less than ten, I will simply reply, "Thank you. What would be your suggestions on how I can improve?"

• I will stop being perceived as overly opinionated. For example, when discussing a topic that I disagree with someone regarding, I will start listening even better by trying to truly understand his or her feelings and opinions, instead of mentally working on a rebuttal. And if someone asks for my opinion, I will start asking questions instead of just giving an answer. This will help me resist sounding emphatic and help other people come up with answers on their own.

• I will start being more proactive about seeking opinions from others who see things differently from me. For example, when moving forward with ideas, I will get input from people who will ask some tough questions.

How Can I Deal with a Bulletproof Person?

To effectively deal with someone like this, it is always important to make sure the person feels validated. Even the extreme of each constraint contains some positives, so make sure you communicate the positives also. Here are some potential strengths to validate: Confident, Self-Assured, Resilient, Independent.

• To persuade them of something, try to make it their idea/decision. Try an approach that includes phrases such as "You expressed something like this a while back, and I totally agreed and have just taken that a step further." Instead of stating your desired end result, ask a question or present a scenario in which they come to the conclusion you are wanting. If they express an opinion, be sure to affirm it and to avoid making emphatic statements such as "That won't work" or "You're wrong on that."

• One of the better ways to deal with people with this constraint is to listen to them, affirm their thinking, and then suggest that you might be able to help them with some additional information. Use this information to help them see when they are wrong or going in the wrong direction, but make it clear that your only goal is for them to be successful. Being adamant or firm with them will rarely work and will likely lead to conflict, which could then cause resentment on your part. Although Bulletproof people are strong willed, this doesn't mean they are bad or malicious people; they just need help sometimes in initially embracing a different perspective.

6 *Killer Constraint #2:* Ostriches (Low Self-Confidence)

Ostriches remind me of Charlie Brown. Okay, I'll admit it—I love Charlie Brown. He's really a good guy who tries hard to be kind to everyone around him. But the fact is that this killer constraint has him by the neck. No one takes him seriously. He can't make eye contact when he gets stressed, and he is incredibly indecisive. He is constantly passed over, even though he has one of the best hearts of the group. Ever thoughtful but never thought about. It has to be discouraging to know that you have talents yet never get a chance to put them to work. The losses that come with this personal constraint are tremendous: lives never fully lived and dreams never tried. I've met quite a few Ostriches over the years, sometimes in the most unexpected arenas, and here's what I want them to do: "Get your head out of the sand!"

The Speed Channel, a cable channel for racing enthusiasts, called my office. Someone there had heard about the results my company was getting in schools and corporations and wanted to find out if the principles of OPC would work in the NASCAR world.

The proposal was simple: together we would choose a NASCAR racing team, and our job was to see if we could make them go faster and perform better on the track after applying our processes for accelerating performance.

The first step was to gather behavioral data on each member of the racing team, including the owners. The team, Fitz/Bradshaw, was owned by Armando Fitz and Terry Bradshaw. We were to work with the Busch Series Navy team, driving the #14 car. I knew very little about NASCAR, even though I had heard a lot about it from my son Micah, who is a racing enthusiast.

But it soon became clear I had much to learn. At my first meeting with the team, one of the guys leaned toward me.

"So, how long have you been working with NASCAR?"

I glanced at my watch. "About twenty minutes."

You can imagine how impressed they were with my credentials. All I knew about their world was that they turned left a lot.

As I started meeting with the team, I was not disappointed. The guys were great to work with, and they loved what they were doing. I didn't have a true appreciation for how tough racing was until I got in the middle of it. The temperatures are unbelievable, and the pace borders on crazy most of the time. Each team in NASCAR goes through an extremely long season, from February to November, with hardly any breaks from week to week.

Because all the races are on weekends, NASCAR takes a huge toll on family life, with divorce rates higher than in many other sports. The schedules are packed, and the competition is fierce.

To add to the pressure, the win ratios for racing are not like any other sport. Each week approximately thirty-two to thirty-six drivers compete in the Busch Series, and there will only be one winner. The competition is not only for winning but also for cumulative points. It's an extremely tough sport, and only a few make it to the top.

Our job was to see if we could improve the Fitz/Bradshaw team's twenty-third-place standing.

We spent some time assessing each of the team members, and we found some indicators of areas that needed further study. The driver, Casey Atwood, was a young man with a lot of heart. He had started racing at fifteen, and by eighteen he was already winning races. Once nicknamed "the next Jeff Gordon," Casey had worked with his crew chief for some time. He was a gifted driver with tremendous natural talent.

So what was the problem? Why were they running only twenty-third in the standings? What were the constraints, and where would we start in the process of improving their speed and performance? These questions were all running through my head.

Losing the Self-Confidence Race

One of my core beliefs is that no group or organization can rise above the constraints of its leadership. On a race team there are several levels of leadership, starting with the owners—and as Terry Bradshaw would jokingly admit, "I'm the biggest constraint on the team." At times he may have been partly right, but not when it came to the actual race. During the race everyone plays a part, but the key players are the driver and the crew chief. The driver is obviously calling the shots from the car. But all of those calls go to the crew chief, who is then expected to make the necessary corrections concerning the car's handling ability and performance on the track. If they can't communicate well with each other, they have a problem.

In the case of the Navy team #14, the crew chief would listen to the driver, Casey Atwood, but he wouldn't necessarily make the changes that Casey requested. Thinking he knew how to correct the problem better, the chief would frequently tell Casey that he *had* made the changes while actually making a different change than what was asked for to see if it improved Casey's performance. In other words the crew chief would second-guess him and make changes that *he* thought Casey needed. Casey never knew his requested changes weren't being made.

It didn't take long before they were speaking two different languages. Casey's confidence was sliding quickly, and soon his slow numbers at the racetrack matched his self-confidence. But that wasn't his only problem. We also knew from the data that his self-control scales were too high at the same time that his self-confidence scales were too low. This produced a risk-averse driver who couldn't take advantage of periodic openings that would normally have given him a lead. It didn't help that Casey wasn't getting the support he thought he was from his crew chief, and all of this was taking a heavy toll on his performance.

We had to raise his self-confidence scales while lowering his self-control scales. This is not too difficult from a behavioral point of view, but the issue was complicated by a third constraint: Casey's resistance to change. Adding confusion to the works was the crew chief, who was telling him that he was doing great, when in fact, he wasn't. Morale and team unity were at a devastating low.

So what did Casey's low self-confidence look like from a behavioral point of view? First, he didn't take chances. What if he wrecked? What if he took a shot at a gap to capitalize on a lead and he hit the wall? After having ridden in the pace car a few times, I have a real appreciation for what that feeling can be like. But going 140 miles per hour in an oval in a pace car is small potatoes—the race cars go between 160 and 185 miles per hour, depending on the track. The entire time you are driving, the super-hot tires are squealing and picking up everything on the track that can stick to them. As you accelerate, whatever debris has stuck to the tires gets hurled at the fender, so you are in sensory overload while trying to avoid a wall that is sometimes inches away. And you're doing all of this in heavy traffic that has only one aim: to pass you or bump you out of the way. It's a little distracting, to say the least.

I could easily understand why a guy wouldn't necessarily want to pass everyone he saw going 180 miles per hour. But that was Casey's job, and it was the crew chief's job to give him the car that would get him to the front.

During one of the races, Armando said, "Tell Casey that I don't care if he brings the car back in a trash bag. Just pass those guys and make something happen." But it didn't happen. True to his Ostrich style, Casey played it safe, and the car came home without a scratch on it.

We also worked on the team's constraints. When we began the process, the pit crew had an in-and-out time of around 16.7–17.5 seconds. As they began to work better together, their times started to drop. They were able to talk through whatever was not working for them as a team when the car pulled in.

Another characteristic of low self-confidence is not being able to capitalize on opportunities. When drivers go into a turn, they will oftentimes stack up as they approach the turn. This means that there could be three cars running neck and neck as they approach the curve. However, it is virtually impossible to go through the curve three cars deep because the guy on the outside of the track has to cover more distance with a worse position to do it from—not to mention the wall coming at you at 160 miles per hour. Going three deep into a curve can easily mean that someone is going to hit the wall.

Usually one driver will back out of the turn and let the other two go through it. The Ostrich will be the one to pick up his foot and let the others go. He will be tentative, holding back when windows open up to pass someone. He will hesitate. Uncertainty is not a good thing at 180 miles per hour, and it doesn't win races.

In addition to his problems on the track, Casey's low self-confidence showed up in other areas. His reluctance to take the lead in meeting and visiting people had a big impact on the sponsors. With the race fans he was great—it was about racing, and he knew his business. With sponsors, however, it was more difficult. He wasn't sure what they needed from him, and his lack of confidence caused him to feel awkward in those situations. Casey was shy by nature, which only complicated things more.

Over time several of the sponsors and their representatives began to feel snubbed by Casey. Although they were mistaking his low self-confidence and shyness for pride and arrogance, it didn't matter; the results were the same. He began losing favor with his sponsors, which is the kiss of death in racing.

Even though Casey was making excellent gains on the track, some of the sponsors began to pressure Armando and Terry for a driver change. Casey was squeezing everything he could from his personal constraints, but they were closing in on him.

Despite Casey's personal struggles, the team did improve. With each week you could see the gains they were making. Terry and Armando (who are great guys to work and hang out with) were gracious in letting us do the work we were doing with the team. And, yes, Terry Bradshaw really is as much fun in person as he is on television.

As the team continued to break through their personal constraints, they rose in the qualifying runs and finishing positions. Within the first three weeks, they had the highest qualifying runs of the team's career. Performance continued to improve over the next few months, and then predictably it leveled off as they hit the ceiling of what their constraints would allow. In this case they went from twenty-third in the standings to twelfth. These were incredible gains for such a short time, and they had every reason to be proud of what they were accomplishing.

Casey was doing his best to perform to the fullest of his constraint scores, but it still wasn't strong enough or soon enough. Between his race performance and the increasing strains with some of the sponsors, Casey's career with Fitz/Bradshaw was coming to a close.

At the end of the day, it didn't matter how gifted or wonderful Casey was as a person; instead it was all about his ability to address his limitations. His constraint of low self-confidence ultimately took the wheel and determined his level of success for him.

Despite his great talents and abilities, Casey's personal constraints cost him his ride with Fitz/Bradshaw.

So where does low self-confidence come from? I don't think we're born with it—I think certain relationships and events shape how we see ourselves. Thinking about the source of this constraint can be helpful.

A Grandfather's Wisdom

Three words changed my life.

When I was twelve, my granddad—a man I loved, respected, and admired—and I were working on our ranch cutting "seeney" beans. I don't know the formal name of these large weeds, but they took over the low-lying parts of the ranch, and we had to cut them by hand because a tractor would get stuck in such a swampy area.

On this particular day it was unusually hot and muggy, and I probably sweated off several pounds. I enjoyed the hard work, but my mind was preoccupied with the Little League baseball game I had pitched the night before. As I talked to my granddad about the game, I explained in detail how I had not pitched well. I had thrown some wild pitches and missed some great opportunities to strike several guys out. My granddad interjected, "Do you know what you're doing?"

"Yes, sir," I answered, "I'm talking about last night's game and how I messed up."

"Son, do you know what you need to do?" he replied, as we both stopped our work and looked directly at each other. He leaned on his brush hook and said the three words I will never forget: "Unpack your bag."

He noticed the obvious question marks floating around in my head, so he continued, "When you stowed your baseballs, your glove, and your bat after the game, you also stowed your failure. You need to unpack your bag so you can be ready for the next game. You're spending all this time looking back. The only thing behind you is your rear end. I've been back there and seen it...and it isn't worth looking at! Learn what you need to learn from the game, then use those lessons to start focusing on tomorrow."

My granddad didn't say much—but when he did, it stuck. I never forgot those words, and to this day I refuse to spend too much time looking back. I definitely want to learn from yesterday, but I am not going to spend time living with regrets and dwelling on "what-ifs." The lesson is simple: you can't run a good race if you are always looking back.

The struggles, conflicts, unmet expectations, insecurities, abuses, difficult relationships, and overwhelming events in life cause all of us to end up with some baggage we need to unpack. The key is to be willing to deal with these emotional wounds because the deeper we stuff those feelings into our bag, the "stinkier" they get. And this baggage can be an overwhelming weight to carry around on a day-to-day basis.

Are You an Ostrich?

Check any of the following symptoms that occur and add up the total.

- ☐ If I make a mistake or disappoint someone, I have a hard time moving on.
- ☐ There are a lot of people more talented than I am.
- ☐ What other people think about me is very important.
- ☐ I am shy and reserved. Meeting new people is hard for me.
- ☐ I give in to strong personalities fairly easily.
- ☐ When someone gives me a compliment, I feel uncomfortable just saying "thank you," so I tend to deflect it.
- ☐ When faced with a new situation, I'm not sure how to proceed without someone else's help and direction.
- ☐ I sometimes find myself internalizing little frustrations and then eventually letting them out all at once.
- ☐ I don't always share my opinions because someone else is probably already thinking the same thing.
- ☐ Conflict is very stressful to me, so I tend to avoid it... sometimes by not saying what I'm really thinking.

Ostrich Tendencies?

Mark your total below.

So I'm an Ostrich—Help Me!

When I sit down to talk to someone who struggles in this area, I sometimes start with something like, "Off the top of your head, go ahead and tell me a bunch of your strengths—the things you really believe you excel at."

They usually bumble around for a minute before I put them out of their misery. Then I process their response and affirm their humility while also encouraging them to genuinely embrace more of their strengths. It's almost as if they look at themselves with blurry glasses on, unable to really see the beauty and talent in the mirror. In fact, your main goal may be to be able to recognize and truly embrace your strengths.

Here's another scenario to think about: If you were working with a kid on a project and the kid was trying really hard but messed up a little, I know exactly how you would react. You'd say, "Come on, get it right, dummy; can't you be more careful? There you go again!" Obviously I'm not being serious, because you would never do that. So if it's not okay to talk to a child that way, why is it okay to talk to yourself that way?

Some of my dearest friends have struggled in this area, and it breaks my heart when I see how they can internalize so much. And as I write this, my mind is drawn back to some of the tougher times in my life when I couldn't stop beating myself up. I want all of us to keep our humility and sensitivity, but let's not let those strengths deteriorate into constraints.

There's no one else like you, so let your voice be heard!

Specific TrAction Steps

Here are some sample action steps you can take to start getting traction—today! Once you read all of the constraint chapters, if this is determined to be one of your killer constraints, then steps like these will be part of your TrAction Plan (to be built in chapter 15).

- I will start embracing my strengths by writing out a list of them, then reading over it daily until they are fully internalized. [You might need to get a trusted friend to help create the list.]

- When I have negative thoughts about myself, I will start replacing them with more truthful ones. So instead of thinking, "I can't believe I spilled that on him...that was so careless...I bet he was really more upset than he showed...I was just trying to help and look what happened," I will substitute this with: "This can happen to anybody, and he knew I was trying to help, and there's really nothing I can do about it at this point, so I'm not going to lose sight of a meaningful dinner."

- I will start a journal by going to a bookstore and purchasing something to write in. I will write down the thoughts I am having about myself and watch the progression over time. [Periodically review the journal with someone you trust who can support you in the growth process.]

- I will stop being perceived as overly needy for affirmation from others. If someone withholds his or her approval, I will step back and objectively decide that I can still move forward. While still being sensitive to what other people think, I will become more self-affirming.

How Can I Deal with an Ostrich?

To effectively deal with someone like this, it is always important to make sure the person feels validated. Even the extreme of each constraint contains some positives, so make sure you communicate the positives also. Here are some potential strengths to validate: Humble, Sensitive, Supportive.

• It is especially important to be sensitive when communicating with people who have this constraint. If you need to challenge them, make sure you are the right person to do so and also realize that their ears are magnified to correction. A great technique to practice is to ask questions to help them see a different way without feeling beat up. Invest in them and earn the right so they will be able to hear you effectively. Always point out the positives in them and their work, motivating them with more of a cheerleader role. Use statements such as "There you go—that's it!" or "Wow, this is great," and try to put them in a position where minimal risk is involved.

• Make an extra effort to listen more to people like this and to try to understand their feelings. Gain a sensitivity to their current state by finding out more about what they have been through. Ask questions such as "Be honest with me—what are you feeling at this point?" and "I really want your feedback—have I said anything that is troubling you?" Remember, someone with self-confidence struggles will likely avoid conflict and hold in their feelings. You will need to probe more than usual to get them to let out what they are thinking.

7 *Killer Constraint #3:* Marshmallows (Overly Nurturing)

Amber, a young college student, is pretty, bright, and comes from a good family. She is kind to everyone, takes in strays, and is a real joy to be around. She also has a boyfriend—a young man who has taken advantage of her in many ways. He is habitually late when he picks her up for a date. He fails to call when he says he will. He forgot her birthday, and last Christmas he asked his mother to pick out a quick gift since he had to rush out to a Christmas Eve party with some guys. After they started living together, she never hesitated to do his laundry or cook for him. She even balances his checkbook!

Amber told me all of this, until she broke down crying and disclosed that her boyfriend had been running around on her. "How can he treat me this way when I am so good to him?" she asked.

"The reason he's treating you so poorly is that he's figured out that a nice person like you won't confront him on his behavior. He takes all you have to give, then goes out to see what else he can get from others who have the same constraints," I said.

Amber gives herself away as though there is an endless supply of her as a person. And there isn't. In fact, many people give themselves completely away, not realizing that a relationship with regular withdrawals but no deposits will ultimately run dry. But this constraint doesn't appear overnight. It starts in childhood with related boundary and self-worth issues.

Too Much of a Good Thing?

Ado Annie from *Oklahoma!* sang that she was "just a girl who cain't say no."

All of us know someone who is renowned for their accommodating nature: the employee who covers everyone else's shifts on holidays and weekends, the mom who cleans up after the entire neighborhood, the friend who lends money to everyone and never gets paid back. We love these selfless givers who make life easier for everyone.

So what's wrong with being a softie?

Overly nurturing people struggle with drawing boundaries. Their nurturing and caregiving behavior goes beyond what is good for them or others. In fact, others come to expect or depend on it to the extent that if you try to change it, they'll often get upset because you aren't being "yourself." They don't want you to change.

Overnurturers can't confront others when something is wrong. My wife, Susan, and I have a friend who has been this way with her kids for years. She has always made excuses for their inappropriate behavior, and when she did correct them, she sounded like she was making an incredible request that was so wrapped in sugar by the time she finally said it, it had lost all meaning. She really thinks that she can love her sons into correct behavior by giving them "freedom" to grow and work through their own misbehaviors.

The problem is that her personal constraint has produced constraints in their lives. Not surprisingly, although they are both over forty years old, they are still irresponsible and selfish. One of them has been married several times, and they are both still struggling to "find themselves." They can't stick with anything, and their mother makes excuses for their shiftlessness by saying that they are just looking for something that they can be good at. It would be more appropriate for her to suggest that they get up in the morning and get a job instead of waiting for their wives to take care of everything. In fact, their wives have taken on many of the responsibilities that their mother handled for years. Neither of the "boys" does anything around the house. "Wife" does it. From mowing the yard, to cooking, to cleaning, to raising their kids—she does it all.

Overly nurturing parents take up too much of the load in raising their family. They do it all. In marriage women usually struggle with this behavior more than men. There are exceptions, but they are just that—exceptions. When one person does everything for others, it encourages selfishness and a sense of entitlement.

For example, a husband and wife could be sitting in the living room watching television, and the nurturing spouse will go to the kitchen to get a drink. He or she will automatically offer the spouse something as well. Yet when the nonnurturing spouse goes to get something, the last thing on his or her mind would be to offer the other person something. Certainly part of this is common courtesy, but at some point, it also emerges as part of an unhealthy pattern.

If a person is thoughtful and considerate, that doesn't qualify as being overly nurturing. But when it goes to the extreme, it becomes a problem.

First, if I extend myself so much for others that I am constantly running behind on my own obligations or I am late coming home or I have committed all of my "extra" time to doing for others, resentments and neglect of core relationships usually arise. Second, healthy relationships are built when people care enough to confront unhealthy behaviors in each other with love. When we give too much in order to "balance out" others' unwillingness to give, we actually hurt them by not allowing them to grow in this area. Many marriages lack a sense of tenderness that is fostered when two people care for the details of each other's well-being.

Being gracious is one thing. Being unable to draw healthy boundaries is another. Oftentimes overnurturers believe that if only they can care for and give enough to others their own needs and desires will be met, and everyone will live happily ever after. Gambling on the premise that life is fair and that their love will save the world, the Marshmallow often has a rude awakening in store regarding the way real life works. But this constraint doesn't appear overnight. It starts in childhood.

Identifying Personal Constraints During Childhood

Is there a way to spot some of these behaviors in children so they can be dealt with years before they develop into full-grown constraints?

Overnurturers often begin as friendly children who lack the ability to draw healthy boundaries or to be self-affirming. I remember seeing this in the young daughter of a friend of mine, a ten-year-old named Carrie. I will often ask children questions to cause them to think a little and to encourage them to answer in self-affirming ways. My little friend was getting in the backseat of her dad's car as the three of us were heading to the store on an errand.

I asked Carrie, "Do you like your hair pulled back the way your mom fixed it?"

"I like it fixed that way if *you* like it," she replied.

To most people this comment would not mean much. But my first thought was "That's interesting; she doesn't have an opinion other than the one that I am going to have." There was more to the story because I also happened to know that she was struggling with her friends at school. Some girls were keeping her out of a group that she had been in, and she was feeling hurt and left out. Carrie's emotional well-being was being dictated by other little girls who were acting mean at the time.

Rather than being dependent on others for their approval, most healthy kids would develop the ability to be self-approving and feel happiness within themselves. Some children, like Carrie, need extra help in learning how to build a strong self-image so others' opinions do not override their own sense of self-acceptance. All of us would like the approval of key people in our lives, but it should never dictate our own views—we need to be able to know that we look nice in a certain outfit or that we are good at something or to celebrate ourselves for some particular thing we know we do well.

How many little girls go through life seeking approval, only to find that others can easily withhold it and, thereby, crush the sweetest of hearts? It is one thing to dance for the pure joy of dancing and quite another to dance with the hope that someone else will approve of the dance. Self-affirmation will help to keep boundaries in place so that, later on, nurturing skills will be balanced by a healthy self-image. Otherwise youngsters will grow up looking for approval anywhere they can get it.

When our boys were young, I would often have them help with repairs and projects around the house and ranch, asking them questions as we worked.

How do you think you did on that paint job? How did you figure out how to solve that problem with the leaky pipe? Did it make you feel good to be able to repair that fence so quickly? How do you feel when you've done a job so well?

These kinds of questions and comments are at the core of teaching others how to self-affirm. Seeing that you've achieved something, then being able to declare it to another person is a healthy exercise for a child. Most people I see have a difficult time affirming their own talents and accomplishments, which can lead to broken boundaries and emotional needs that result in a search for acceptance through overgiving and overnurturing.

Toasted Marshmallows

In business it looks much the same. The overnurturers are always the ones who do everything. They stay late, they work on projects to help others, they burn the candle at both ends, and they never say no. When their work schedule is full, they still take on more. Being Marshmallows, they are soft and sweet, with no ability to resist unreasonable requests or to "just say no." Even if they're asked at the last hour for help with a project that is in a crisis due to someone else's irresponsibility, the overnurturer will almost always cancel his or her own schedule to rescue someone in need.

Overnurturers rarely make good managers because they can't say anything negative. Any feedback or input is couched in terms that overlook poor performance. The stakes go up when a Marshmallow manager coddles employees at the expense of his or her responsibility to the company's success.

At my company there is a policy that you don't speak negatively to others about someone on your team. But what happens when you are promoted and you must give critical feedback so others can grow? Overly nurturing people really struggle with giving negative feedback to others, even when it is required of them. They believe that continuous encouragement will be enough to get the other person where he or she needs to go. In many cases that is simply not true.

Some of you (especially the Marshmallows!) will say, "Flip, what's wrong with being helpful or willing to go the extra mile?" The answer to that would be nothing, if it is a response to a true emergency or occasional need. But if you find yourself regularly picking up after others, filling in for irresponsible people, or having your time and energy used up on other people's poor planning or continual crises, you need to come to terms with the fact that you may be a Marshmallow (remember, they are soft and sweet, but that doesn't mean they're healthy for everyone!).

You don't have to turn into a Critic, which we will look at in the next chapter, but you do have to choose *balance* in your giving and tending to others. Ultimately the most loving thing you can do for others is to help them grow—to encourage, teach, and sometimes admonish others so that they can move beyond their personal constraints and become all that they were destined to become.

Are You a Marshmallow?

Check any of the following symptoms that occur and add up the total.

- ☐ Given enough time, people will usually correct their own mistakes.
- ☐ If someone at work is feeling down or needs personal help, they tend to come to me for encouragement.
- ☐ It is more important to listen to someone's problems than to finish a task at work.
- ☐ I sometimes say what the other person wants to hear rather than what I am really thinking.
- ☐ It's hard for me to be a tough disciplinarian.
- ☐ People's feelings are extremely important to me, and because of this I sometimes even bail people out from situations they've created.
- ☐ I have a hard time saying no to people.
- ☐ I routinely find myself overcommitted to various responsibilities.
- ☐ I would have a hard time saying something that might hurt someone else, even if it really needed to be said.
- ☐ At times I feel like people take advantage of my being willing to help.

Marshmallow Tendencies?

Mark your total below.

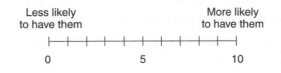

So I'm a Marshmallow—Help Me!

I really try to be careful in discussing this constraint because it is difficult to tell someone who is very kind and nurturing that they may be slightly out of balance. So first of all I applaud those of you who are very nurturing, and I hope you continue to build up and encourage those around you.

Here's a thought to consider: I'm sure all of us remember the announcement the steward or stewardess makes when you first sit down on an airplane (that is, before your back starts aching and your knees lock!): "In case of an emergency, oxygen masks will descend from the ceiling. Please put on your mask first and then assist those around you." There is a reason you are to put yours on first: if you have your mask on, you'll be able to better help those you care about. I think some of you are so busy tending to everyone else that every once in a while you wake up and your tank is empty. So let's make sure we fill our own tank, too! This may sound selfish on the surface, but it's really not.

A lot of times just being able to say NO is one of the key issues. I work with several people who struggle with this at times. The saying we have about this is: "No is not a negative." If I always say no, then, of course, *I'm* the negative part of this equation, but sometimes saying no is the best choice.

Is my goal to tell you what to do in every situation? Or to harden you? Or, even worse, to make you selfish? Definitely not. My goal is to simply help all of us find the right balance. Sometimes I am very patient and understanding, and other times I decide to enforce appropriate consequences. This obviously gets tricky because we all want black-and-white answers, but I'm not here to provide those. I'll simply challenge you to evaluate yourself, to get feedback from those who know you well, and to investigate if it would benefit you and those around you to tackle this constraint.

Specific TrAction Steps

Here are some sample action steps you can take to start getting traction—today! Once you read all of the constraint chapters, if this is determined to be one of your killer constraints, then steps like these will be part of your TrAction Plan (to be built in chapter 15).

• I will start enforcing consequences appropriately. If I am tempted to let someone off the hook or bail them out, I will make sure I am doing what is in everyone's best interest. I will start being known as someone who cares about people enough to hold them accountable. As hard as this can be for me, I know it will actually allow some relationships to deepen.

• I will start saying no when appropriate. I won't stop being kind and helping others, but I will avoid overcommitting or wearing myself out in the process. Along the same lines I will stop doing things for people that they should do for themselves. The reality is that people are prone to take advantage of me, so being strong in this area can help me avoid setting any dangerous precedents.

• I will be more proactive about tending to myself. I'll be able to give more if my tank is full, so I will mark time on my calendar to do something I enjoy.

• I will start speaking up with feedback more frequently. If someone asks my opinion, I can be diplomatic but also completely honest. I need to be willing to challenge those around me and call them to a high but fair standard.

How Can I Deal with a Marshmallow?

To effectively deal with someone like this, it is always important to make sure the person feels validated. Even the extreme of each constraint contains some positives, so make sure you communicate the positives also. Here are some potential strengths to validate: Caring, Encouraging, Appreciative, Relational.

• To be heard by and to connect with Marshmallows, be sure to applaud the motive behind the nurturing behavior. Their concern for others is a great asset, so be careful of giving the impression you don't value this trait.

• Try to put these people in a position to capitalize on their tendencies. For example, putting a Marshmallow in a role that requires giving tough feedback to people wouldn't be ideal. Similarly, standing up to a dominant personality could be difficult for them, so have realistic expectations. Drawing boundaries is more difficult for them, so encourage them to take steps that are small and appropriate.

8 *Killer Constraint #4:* Critics (Too Demanding, Nitpicky, or Harsh)

I was invited to a meeting some months ago with the leadership of a successful company involved in land development, construction, and sales. The grounds were beautifully manicured. As I walked into the building, I was greeted and taken to the second-floor offices that overlooked a peaceful pond setting. The entire scene was permeated with an aura of elegance and understated success. I was enjoying myself and getting settled in when the rest of the group joined us for the meeting. About ten of us were in the meeting, and things were going well with the presentation.

A Climate of Fear

Shortly after we began the discussion segment, a forty-something woman named Pam raised questions about some of the material that was being presented.

Suddenly, the positive atmosphere crumbled. Without any warning she said, "This is ridiculous. Who prepared these numbers?"

"Whoa . . . what was that?" I thought to myself. "This is going to be interesting."

The meeting abruptly changed in both tone and content. There was a brief response, and then more rapid-fire questions from Pam. As I observed everyone in the room begin to tense up, Pam continued to plow ahead with utter disregard for the anxiety and animosity she was creating in the meeting. To make matters worse she wasn't even listening to the responses of several of the other participants. Because she was not listening, she was missing important information that would have answered several of her questions.

A few more minutes went by, and the person who had called the meeting asked for a short break. I sat quietly while the team leader tried to discuss with Pam what was taking place.

Pam just shook her head and crossed her arms, refusing to listen to him. Finally, the frustrated team leader said, "Pam, *why are you pushing like this?*"

Her response was classic. "They don't ever listen to me, and I am tired of being ignored. I am always telling them things they don't want to hear, and they don't get it. They must be stupid." The message came across loud and clear. Pam was harsh and critical, and she had unloaded on the group both in private and in public for some time. Now she was going one step further and berating them in the presence of their boss.

Pam's critical nature was legendary. It turned her meetings into fear-filled gatherings of faultfinding and blame. The entire culture of the company was affected by her behavior, and many of the better employees were leaving the company because their own integrity would not allow them to stay and work under such constant duress. Others were searching for ways to transfer out of her department. The climate had become one of fear and anxiety as the employees awaited her next assault.

Pam's boss asked me to meet with her later that day.

After the door was shut and the chairs arranged so we could face each other comfortably, I asked her point-blank, "Does this work for you?"

She was somewhat confused at first and said, "Do you mean the seating in here? Or the meeting?"

"Well, the meeting is what I'm thinking about," I responded.

Pam immediately became defensive. She launched into a rant about the problems that had been going on for some time, which she knew wouldn't get any better. She also had plenty to say about how the others didn't work as hard as they should and didn't have the same commitment that she had and "besides, they really don't know what I know about the situation anyway."

Pam's monologue was filled with venom and bitterness. It was obvious she had outlived her effectiveness in her position. For years she had been critical of others, and now she was way past trying to be tactful about it. Her corporate career was over in this company unless she took some drastic steps to salvage her crumbling position.

Sadly, in her mind she was being insightful and helpful by pointing out what was not working. In truth she was being highly critical and frequently abusive of others. In her opinion no one, and I mean no one, could do it as well as she could. She was relentless. Pam's criticism ran throughout the company, and she would as easily pick out the faults of the company president as she would the janitor. Every decision, every strategy, every plan, every report, every hiring decision, every acquisition *all* had flaws that only she could see.

Even more telling was the personal side of Pam's life. She had gone through a divorce, and her only child was estranged from her. She had no close friends and would tell you that she didn't have time for friends because she was too busy with her career. She was critical of others and their work. Yet the job that she served so completely was about to be taken from her. Pam was asked to resign a few days later.

How many people do we all know who act this way? These naysayers believe their job is to point out all the flaws of an idea or project or, worse, the people they work with.

There is no virtue in finding fault with everyone else's work or contribution. There *is* great virtue, however, in finding both goodness and growth opportunities within someone and helping them grow to become their best. Every day companies are faced with the question of what to do with baggage-packing employees—those who come with unresolved issues from their past that continually get played out in their present.

"Do we keep someone who is a competent person but is harsh in dealing with others? Do we make exceptions for their inappropriate behavior in order to keep the benefit of their skill set?"

Maybe for the short term but not for long. If a poorly behaving employee refuses help in correcting a problem, it is only a matter of time before his or her contributions are outweighed by constraints. That's when bosses get fired by management... or subordinates start to leave for greener pastures.

I worked for a man with the same constraints as Pam when I was in college. One summer I went to work on a surveying crew. Bob, the man who ran the surveying department, was a perfectionist, and he expected everything to be exactly right all the time. He was also cynical and sarcastic, and during the time I worked for him, I never once heard him say anything good about anyone or another's work.

One of his former employees had gone into the army and was now returning home, and Bob was giving him his old job back. I had listened to Bob talk about his favorite hand, Billie, for weeks. I was curious as to what Billie would be like, since I had never before seen Bob pleased with anything. "This guy must walk on water," I thought.

A week later Billie showed up and started working for Bob again. Day after day we worked, and finally, it happened. The three of us were together in Bob's truck when Bob blew up at Billie with a list of complaints as long as my arm. He insisted the army had ruined Billie, that he didn't know how to work anymore, he didn't care about quality, he didn't do his job, and on and on. When we pulled up at the engineering office, Billie and I stayed in the truck while Bob went into the office to get something.

After a few minutes Billie looked over at me and said, "I have tried to put up with Bob and his criticism before. I thought I could do it, because I needed the job. But I can't stand it. I'm leaving." With that he got out of the truck that we had just ridden to work in, walked to the curb, stuck his thumb out, and hitchhiked the forty miles back to his home.

When Bob came out and got in the truck, he said, "Where's Billie?" I told him what happened, and he didn't say a word for the rest of the day.

Let me share something personal that really played into what happened later that week. The next day Bob was at it again, and I was the only hand he had. I had already worked more than fifty hours that week, and it was only Thursday. We had two more days of work to go for that week alone. That afternoon as we were getting in the truck, Bob lit into me about something that he wasn't pleased with—and he spared no effort to humiliate me.

What was one of the personal constraints hindering my life at that time? I had a terrible problem with conflict. In fact, because of my rough childhood and how I had been treated at home, I was honestly afraid of conflict and didn't know how to handle it. What would happen if I said something and got fired, or worse? I had always avoided conflict and would never have spoken up for myself.

Except for this day.

I was tired, I was hungry, and Bob made the mistake of saying something about my girlfriend. That was it.

Our two personal constraints collided.

Right there I told him, "You're the meanest old man I have ever met. You can't keep help because you are impossible to work with, and all you do is bellyache about everything. It's no wonder no one wants to work for you. You've never kept anyone for longer than six months, and you have been doing this all of your miserable life. You don't even get along with your own family. One more word out of you and *I quit!*"

Well, there it was. I had finally had it. My heart was pounding, and I was a nervous wreck on the inside, but I had done it! I was glad I hadn't had time to think about it, or I would have talked myself out of saying anything. I got back in the truck, and he didn't say another word for the entire day.

The next day Bob came to me and said, "I apologize for yester-day. I told my wife what happened, and she agreed with you. I won't do that again, I promise." That was that, and he never talked to me that way again. We were friends until he died. Sadly, there weren't a lot of people at his funeral, since he had alienated most everybody during his lifetime. Critics generally end up lonely.

Critics at Home

And that's the tragedy of Critics—their personal constraints are even more hurtful at home. Nothing is ever good enough. You hear it when they walk in the door. If the children have done the dishes, an overly critical person will ask, "Why didn't you wipe off the countertops?"

You can't really please them, and sadly, they usually don't have any idea how critical they come across to others. In their mind they are just stating the obvious or being helpful. Critics don't see what they are doing, and when it gets pointed out to them, they still can't see it unless you approach them with a series of specific examples so the picture is crystal clear.

In some cases people make a living being overly critical. In certain professions being overly critical is a good thing. For example, in engineering you need someone with a critical eye who pays a lot of attention to detail to catch things that aren't right. But take that same mind-set home and see how well it plays with your family.

Donnie was a client of mine who owned a large engineering firm. He had been one of the founding partners, and he "knew" what had to be done. He claimed his other partners didn't work as hard as he did, and they didn't see the whole picture like he could. In addition, he said the young engineers they were hiring didn't have the same work ethic, and he couldn't find good help anymore because of the way young people are today.

One day we were walking into the building, and he began complaining about the poor job that someone was doing with the lawn and flowers. When we got to his secretary, he told her to get another lawn-care company if this one couldn't get the job done right. He was tired of sloppy work, and at least he shouldn't have to look at it in his own building.

She looked up and said, "Donnie, don't you remember? Your son is doing the lawn for the summer. He just started this week."

"Well, tell him to get it right. He can't do it here like he does it at home," he barked as he turned and walked into his office.

What a bear. Nothing and no one made him happy. Finally, with the aid of his partners, we isolated him in a job that didn't impact people and then overpaid the two people who did report to him. The other partners called it "hazardous duty" pay and were happy to pay it. They felt it was well deserved just for trying to deal with him.

Looking, But Not Seeing

Dealing with overly critical personalities is a constraint I'm intimately familiar with because I've been faced with it my whole life in the form of some of the people nearest and dearest to me—my own family.

Years ago, as I was finishing my graduate program, I knew I wanted to do something different with my life than other people around me. I had to do something that counted for more than just doing business or getting a job. After much thought and soul-searching, as I mentioned earlier I decided to start a nonprofit counseling center that would serve anyone who walked in the door looking for help.

I drove down to see my parents with mixed feelings about what to say about my future. I was excited about it, and I didn't want them to dampen those feelings with their own. For years they'd had their own plans for me—plans that did *not* include mingling with the poor and destitute of central Texas. That night after dinner we sat in the living room, and I shared with them that I wasn't going to Africa on a prestigious research assignment after all. Instead I was planning to work locally with gang members and troubled kids.

Their reaction of shock and disappointment was almost more than I could bear. They were quick to tell me I was throwing my life away and to let me know what a disaster it would all be. "How are you going to survive?" they asked. "You're going to starve to death, and so is your family. This is a terrible decision—who's going to support you?"

These criticisms weren't new to me. I had heard them with every new idea I had ever tried growing up. But even though I was a responsible adult this time, the response from my mother was the same as it had always been. She could not see what I was talking about nor why my decision was important to me.

Well, I did open the clinic, and it was enormously fulfilling work. Years later, after newspaper articles, gubernatorial appointments, awards, and recognition, I thought my mother would finally see that what I was doing was good and important. But she never did. Over the years I think I gave up on her understanding me or my future and began to focus on doing what I thought I was supposed to do with my life. It was simply too time consuming to try to get her approval, and if I am completely honest, it was too painful as well.

New Life for an Old Barn

Many years later, after I had left the nonprofit and started a new company, Susan and I were visiting Vermont and met some wonderful people. At dinner that night (we were staying at a bed and breakfast), a new friend asked what we had done during the day. I told him that I had spent the afternoon looking at old barns—but they were all going by at seventy miles an hour, since the group I was riding with was not anxious to stop and let me wander through every old barn in Vermont. Jim and Marilyn Ellis, a young couple from Ohio, were sitting across from me, and one of them asked why I was so fascinated with old barns.

I said, "Well, I would like to take one down, haul it to Texas, and build my office out of it." Marilyn's eyes twinkled, and she said, "That's interesting. I have a barn in Ohio that is more than one hundred seventy years old and in mint condition. I would be happy to give it to you if you could use it."

It was all I could do to keep from jumping up and running around the table.

"Yep, that will work," I replied.

And it did.

After planning a thousand steps, I hired a crew to take it down in what turned out to be one of the worst snowstorms in Ohio history. The two-story, four-bay barn slid its way across the Northeast to head south for warmer weather in Texas. When the truck finally arrived, the boys and I stood there in disbelief.

We were looking at forty-eight thousand pounds of beams and posts.

I will never forget the feeling that came over us as we lifted those hand-hewn ten-inch-by-ten-inch-by-forty-foot oak beams that the Amish had cut and shaped 170 years earlier. We unloaded each and every beam and then stacked them into assigned piles.

A few weeks after the beams arrived, I decided to have an old-fashioned barn raising to put up the main timbers. On a hot Texas summer weekend, I invited about thirty buddies of mine over to reconstruct the barn.

There is a reverence that you can feel when you touch something that was made by someone who took pride in their work. That afternoon each of us took an old peg home with us to remind us of the amazing craftsmanship of the barn and the time we had together that day.

A few weeks into the building process, my mother came to visit us for several days. My oldest son, Matthew, was climbing around on the beams of the building to scrape and clean them up for the next steps in the construction. He was lying on one of the highest beams like a big tabby cat, watching the world play out around him, when my mother walked up.

She came into the barn, turned to me with a familiar look, and said, "This doesn't look like it's going to work. Your clients aren't going to come all the way out here to see you. Before long you'll go broke and lose everything. Then what will you do?"

And then she finally said what I had known she had been thinking for most of my life: "Flip, why can't you be a normal person with a normal job and live like everyone else?"

I stood there looking around at the beams and spotted my son lying high up in the rafters. He had heard everything. I quietly said to her, "Well, it will be a heck of a place to store hay, won't it?" Shaking her head, she walked back to the air-conditioned house.

After she was out of earshot, Matthew asked me a question I will never forget.

"Pop, how did you grow up hearing that all the time?"

My first thought was "What do you mean?" He continued, "She is always so negative to you, and you don't even seem to hear it."

I knew things were different in that relationship than with any other relationship in my life. But it was at that moment that I realized that even as my mother had lost her ability to see things in *me,* I had lost my ability and desire to hear things from *her.*

It was better for me not to hear her critical complaints and instead choose to listen to others who could "see" the things that ultimately made my life what it is. I might not have made it had it not been for the positive people in my life. For sure I wouldn't be where I am today.

Are You a Critic?

Check any of the following symptoms that occur and add up the total.

- ☐ I notice things that are not right or as good as they could be.
- ☐ Sarcasm is a style of humor that I can relate to.
- ☐ Other people often fail to live up to my high expectations.
- ☐ People don't seem genuinely excited or happy to see me.
- ☐ I get frustrated easily if other people don't give me what I want in the way I want it.

☐ I've been accused of being a skeptic by people who know me well.

☐ I'm not really complaining, I'm just pointing out problems that should be fixed.

☐ I've been known to give people feedback that wasn't asked for.

☐ I don't give top scores because there's always room for improvement.

☐ I tend to notice the quirks that other people have.

Critic Tendencies?

Mark your total below.

Less likely to have them   More likely to have them

0   5   10

So I'm a Critic—Help Me!

I met with someone recently who struggled in this area, and as we were talking, I noticed a pen sitting on his desk. I reached over and picked it up, gripped it tightly with both hands, and bent it in the middle. Then I set the pen back in front of him and said, "That's what you do to your talents. Every time you pick at people, you undermine your own abilities. Take this pen with you as a reminder—and by the way, no extra charge for that." He was amused, but more important, he got the point.

I don't mind the fact that people like this are able to notice room for improvement in people and in processes. I just want to make sure they earn the right to vocalize their opinions. I'll be honest; I'm not a big fan of others trying to fix me. Instead of fixing people, how about investing in them? Fixing sounds entirely too quick and one sided, while investing implies long-term responsibility from both parties.

A neat illustration of the dangers of this trait can be made using a simple aluminum can. Take a soft-drink can and put a dent in it each time you catch yourself offering an unsolicited opinion, making a sarcastic comment, or complaining about something. Then try to bend the can back to its original shape. You just can't do it.

If you are in a position of overseeing others, this is critically important to tackle. But don't take my word for it. Listen to the research that repeatedly shows that when people quit jobs, in most cases they are actually quitting their bosses. And for parents, similar research shows that kids of perfectionists are destined to have a fear of failure.

So instead of seeing what everyone else needs to change, focus more on what people are good at. Invest in them and earn the right to challenge them. Think of the talent within them that you are hoping to unleash. Maybe that's what Michelangelo was thinking when he said, "I saw an angel in the stone and carved to set it free."

Specific TrAction Steps

Here are some sample action steps you can take to start getting traction—today! Once you read all of the constraint chapters, if this is determined to be one of your killer constraints, then steps like these will be part of your TrAction Plan (to be built in chapter 15).

• I will stop expecting too much from people. My high expectations for others can create the perception that I am difficult to please. When I am too hard on someone, I will apologize even if I think he or she is being hypersensitive. I will identify three people and ask them, "Are my expectations difficult to meet?" and if they say yes, I will apologize and affirm them.

• To stop complaining as much, I will go a full day without making a single complaint. Whether it's a family member, friend, coworker, or fast-food employee, I won't say anything negative and instead will think about why they feel and act the way they do. Further, I will start focusing more on the positives in people, situations, and ideas.

• I will stop giving people feedback that wasn't asked for. Instead of being the feedback police, I will be willing to let others who know the person say some of those things; otherwise I may be further seen as a Critic. I will also have the patience to realize that I might not always be right, so it may be worth holding back my opinion for now.

• I will start watching my body language more closely. I will be more expressive and positive in my comments and tone, without crossing my arms or furrowing my brow. It never hurts to smile!

• I will stop taking subtle jabs at people or using sarcasm. It's really not worth the laugh, and people are unlikely to tell me if they are offended or hurt.

How Can I Deal with a Critic?

To effectively deal with someone like this, it is always important to make sure the person feels validated. Even the extreme of each constraint contains some positives, so make sure you communicate the positives also. Here are some potential strengths to validate: Discerning, High expectations, Sees areas of improvement.

• When interacting with a nitpicker, be sure to make statements such as "I can see that you have some reservation and may see some challenges," "That's incredible insight—what a great point," "We really need to weigh these concerns heavily," and "I really hear you, I'm just trying to piece everything together."

• If you are feeling nitpicked by someone like this, try not to take it personally because it may not be about you. Be willing to speak up and say, "I'm feeling a little overwhelmed, so it would help me if you could point out some positives too."

9 *Killer Constraint #5:*
Icebergs (Low Nurturing)

Karen Hart was a teacher who had attended one of my company's Capturing Kids' Hearts educator trainings. Students called her Mrs. Hart—at least when she was around. She discovered that most students called her Mrs. Hart*less* when discussing her among themselves. She couldn't be too upset, as she secretly knew that there was something to the nickname.

The truth, however, is that Karen really *did* love people. At home she was a poster mom for encouragement, affection, and support. But at school she thought that the only way she could command respect and maintain control was by force. She wasn't overly demanding or harsh like the Critics of the previous chapter, but her classroom was not a nurturing place.

She never accepted excuses and didn't want to be too friendly because she believed that students were waiting to take advantage of teachers like that. In many observable ways, she appeared to run the perfect system. Her students turned their work in on time, were never sent to the office, and made adequate academic progress. She received praise from her principal, parents, teachers, and even some students. "I was consistently honored by fellow staff members, and was even nominated for a prestigious teaching award. The signals

I was receiving all reinforced that I must be doing something right," she told me.

To many people Karen was a good teacher. Her kids were compliant, well-behaved, and they scored well on standardized tests. But there was one thing they weren't—which was *connected.*

Although Karen was good at the academic side of teaching, she was not as good at the relational side. As a result she was not only aloof from her students, but she didn't create an environment that was conducive to their connecting to each other, either.

She told me how our training had shown her the personal constraints that were holding her back in the classroom. After the training she dedicated herself to showing more of her nurturing side at school. She complimented kids more often, wrote more notes of encouragement, was more expressive and affirming, and also greeted them as they came into her room. In her words, "Because of what I learned, I was better able to connect with my students and model what healthy, nurturing behavior looks like. I learned how to be really *there* for my students."

At the end of the school year, Karen reflected on the year and her new disciplinary approach. She remembered the stunned faces of her students as she shook their hands for the first time, along with the surprising love she felt (and lump of emotion in her throat) as she realized how much she would miss everyone.

A couple of years ago, I received a letter from a similar teacher named Tara, who decided to tackle this constraint:

> What happened in the last few days of school changed me—
> and changed a lot of other people too. Our grade level was
> going on a field trip to participate in a team-building pro-
> gram called Ropes. Tina had a doctor appointment, and her
> dad was bringing her to join us later that morning.
>
> I saw Tina arrive with her dad and went to greet them.
> Meanwhile, our class was all huddled together, intent on

conquering the next problem facing them. The group had already experienced some significant bonding, so I felt bad that Tina had missed out on some powerful activities. It can be awkward to join a group in the middle of activities like this, especially for a shy kid like Tina who doesn't like to stick out.

As Tina and I approached the class, I shouted enthusiastically (I didn't usually shout or get too excited, but I was trying to be more nurturing and expressive), "Heyyyyy, everybody, Tina is here!"

I had no idea how everyone would respond.

Without hesitation, the entire class—every single student—surrounded her and started yelling, "Yea, Tina's here, Tina's here!" They were jumping up and down, welcoming her back. Even the instructor of our group joined in and, while bowing as if to a queen, said, "Miss Tina has arrived!"

As I realized the significance of that moment to Tina, I turned to see if her dad had seen it, too. With a big smile on his face, he waved and drove away. Later, Tina's dad—with great emotion—told me how much that moment meant to him and Tina's mom. It was a "golden moment" for all of us.

Children often don't realize how much their words and actions mean, but on this special day my kids gave a gift that Tina's dad and I will never forget. The words and actions of my students toward their teammate came from their hearts, and it was a direct result of what I had shared—and modeled—throughout the year.

Karen and Tara loved the kids enough to be willing to change the areas that hindered them as their guide and role model. They may have thought they were making the changes for them, but the lasting impact on their teaching styles and ability to relate to each year's incoming students was a personal reward they had not expected.

Fly the Chilly Skies

In Karen's case she had basically been taught she wasn't supposed to be nurturing at school with her students. That is unfortunate, but not unusual. My company is the largest teacher-educator company in North America, and I hear this all the time. It is a common theme that is shared around the faculty lounges that "teachers aren't supposed to smile till Christmas" or that "you're not the students' *friend*—you're their *teacher*." It is no wonder that many of our kids today don't want to go to school. What child wants to be around people who are not caring or happy to see them or who act as though they don't want them there? The good news is that this is not true of the majority of educators.

I used the example of Karen Hart for two reasons. First, she is now on our staff and does an incredible job working with educators. And second, I wanted to show that in some cases the behavior you see may be tied more to environment and expectations than personal makeup.

However, real Icebergs are a different group entirely. They don't connect well with people and generally don't feel the need to concern themselves with the feelings or well-being of others. I'm not talking about being shy, which is a different constraint. I'm describing people who feel little connectivity or warmth toward others and who go through life tending to business but not people. They can be distant, demanding parents, and they make tough, detached bosses.

You can find many of them in the workplace.

Workplace culture is fascinating. Some companies, like Southwest Airlines, value relationships and are warm, friendly places to work. From the start Southwest created a nurturing culture by design, and they have proven that putting people first *works*. I remember enjoying my first flight with them and being impressed with the teamwork—the pilots were working right along with the flight attendants to quickly clean the cabin for the oncoming passengers.

I also remember another airline that I use quite often because it flies out of the small airport in my town. I was making my connection in a major city, and the captain of the plane was standing next to the check-in counter. The ticket agent asked the captain if he knew whether the plane was ready for boarding, and he gave her a harsh look and pointed to the stripes on the sleeve of his jacket. He snarled, "Do I look like someone who should answer that question? Don't ask me things you should know!" as he stormed off. All the passengers preparing to board heard what he said and looked sympathetically at the young attendant, who was fighting back tears as he walked away. I don't think there was one of us who wanted to get on that plane.

Icebergs Create Igloos

They had filled out their forms and were waiting for me as I stepped out of my office to greet them. Barbara, my secretary at the time, had welcomed the young couple and made them comfortable with the process of seeing a psychotherapist.

As they entered the office, I noticed that the husband waited for his wife to pick the seat she wanted and then he sat down in the chair next to her. They were young and appeared to be career-oriented people who had come to my office straight from work. As we began to go over their information, I noticed that they hadn't filled out the section about why they wanted to see me. That usually meant that there was something that they wanted to talk about privately and didn't want someone to see it on their form. I totally understood and explained to them how confidentiality worked and that they could be assured I would not discuss their concerns with anyone.

After a few general questions I asked, "So, what brings you to see me? How can I help you?" They looked at each other, and Tim, the husband, didn't say a word. His wife, Caroline, looked back at me and said, "He isn't happy with our sex life, and we need to talk about it."

We were off to a great start. He was already somewhat embarrassed, and she was more open about the subject and willing to discuss it head-on. I covered the basic questions: "Are you able to talk about it between yourselves? How do you feel about talking about it? Have you tried to discuss your differences with anyone else, such as someone from your church, an older married couple, or perhaps a friend?"

They both began to relax and shared that they had not been sexually active with other people prior to their marriage and that their relationship was the first for both of them. Tim then said, "I don't think she likes making love with me. I have tried everything I know to be nice, and patient, but I just don't think she cares."

At that point Caroline responded, "It's not that. I do love you, but I just don't have the same needs that you have. You're a man and I'm not. It's different. Tim, you always seem so needy. You just expect too much."

That brought us to an important question. "Tell me—what is *too much?* How often do you make love, on average?"

Tim shared that his work took him away from home for a few days most weeks and he missed Caroline when he was gone. "I call home, and we talk and we enjoy being together because we have the same interests and like to talk about work and things like that."

"Okay, I get the idea that you guys enjoy each other, but that didn't answer the question. How often, on average, do you make love?"

Caroline responded, "Well, on average, about two to three times."

"Two to three times—what? Per month, per day, per week, per year? How often are we talking about?" I asked.

"Maybe two or three times every six months," she responded. Tim looked at me like he was going to break inside.

"Tim, does that sound about right to you?" I asked.

"Yeah, it does, but that's not the only thing about it. She doesn't even hug me when I come home. There are always papers from work piled up in bed with her, and I come in and she speaks and we talk—but that's it. We don't kiss or touch, and she isn't affectionate. I don't run around on her and would never do that, but I want her to love me, and she just doesn't." The hurt in his eyes was truly sad as he expressed his pain as best he knew how. He didn't appear angry, just broken.

"But I do love him, and he knows I love him. I just don't have to go around showing it all the time. It's not that important to me. I can live without all the mushy stuff. I don't want him unhappy, but I don't get it. What's wrong with us having sex every few months? Isn't that all right if that's what we want?"

Of course it's all right—if that is what two people agree to and they are both happy in the relationship. There are no set schedules that all couples have to abide by. From a clinical point of view and out of respect for the couples I may be seeing, I agree that it is up to them, as it should be. However, that was not the case here. Tim was *not* happy, and he was struggling with the lack of affection and nurturance in the relationship as much as he was the absence of sex. Maybe he was struggling with the lack of lovemaking more than the affection, but the point was he was needing more of both.

Over the next few months, we made great progress, but it wasn't the type of progress that I was pleased with. Rather than growing in nurturing and affectionate behaviors, Caroline needed a set routine of behaviors that she could remember to perform with Tim when he came home from work or from out of town. She carried out those behaviors with the regularity of a clock. But obviously something was missing.

Tim eventually had to adjust to Caroline's lack of affection, and for many years he lived a life of quiet "incompletion," taking whatever comfort he could in the friendship and companionship they shared in so many other areas. My relationship with them changed, and they became friends that I would run into every so often. They had a daughter named Tammy who was a joy to be around, and I had the chance to watch her grow up, as well.

One day I got a call from Tammy. She asked if I would do her a great favor and speak to a group of young people at her college when I had an opening in my schedule. She also wanted to buy me lunch. Tammy was as sweet a young lady as I knew, and Susan and I had grown to truly love her. I agreed to lunch, and we looked forward to seeing each other.

We set the lunch date and met at a local restaurant. We enjoyed catching up and sharing stories; then, after we had visited for a while, she gave me a troubled look.

"What's wrong with Mom?" she asked. "Why can't she love me? I come home from school and she doesn't even look like she missed me. I know she loves me, but do you know she never hugs me? And what's really sad is that she is more affectionate to me than she is to Dad." Tammy leaned toward me and quietly asked, "Have I done something, or was there something wrong when I was a kid that made her not want to be around me?"

Wham! There it was. The constraint was still there, and now it was wounding the second most important relationship in her life. I talked with Tammy and let her know that it had nothing to do with her. It was a bit of a balancing act to talk about the subject without saying anything to reveal the discussion I had had with her parents many years before. After a while Tammy looked at me and said, "Flip, I don't want to be that way. I am affectionate with people. I want people to know that I care for them. Mom makes a great corporate person but she doesn't get it as a parent. I need her love, and I need for her to be able to show it. I can tell you one thing: I will not go through my life that way."

Not addressing things that need to be addressed does not result in the problem going away. It's also not enough for others to "adjust" to how you are. Eventually our personal constraints catch us. Sometimes it's too late, and the cost is too high.

A Party for Williams

Mike Steele flew into town to meet with me about Agate, his company headquartered in Texas. Agate is a division of a Fortune 500 company. In addition to being a business leader, Mike has an imposing physical presence as well, standing at over six feet four inches.

I liked him instantly. Mike knew what he was doing and what he wanted. He wanted his company to be the best it could be, and he felt that we could help it get there. As we talked about personal constraints, Mike quickly saw that he had some. In fact, he had several.

He also had an employee who was brilliant, and Mike wanted him to grow as well, so we began our OPC (Overcoming Personal Constraints) processes with both of them.

Mike's number-two person and CFO at Agate was a young man named Hal Williams. He was extremely bright and hardworking, with thick, black-rimmed glasses and a "by-the-numbers" mentality. He was a black-and-white guy when it came to the rules, even the un-written ones. Hal was also quite invested in his own personal career. But he had some serious personal constraints, and as he progressed in the company, these constraints were beginning to have an adverse effect on his progress.

As Mike, his boss, continued to grow, he was offered a position at the parent company headquarters in Dallas as group president. This was a fabulous promotion, and it fulfilled one of the goals we had set when he began our processes. It also meant that Hal was being pro-moted to president of Agate.

Mike's promotion was a highly celebrated event, but Hal's was not. Few if any people celebrated Hal's promotion. His greatest per-sonal constraint was his lack of nurturing and concern for his co-workers. He was involved in those things that meant the most to him rather than the things that meant the most to his employees.

Hal called me that week, and we talked about how he was feel-ing. "Flip, I'm excited about my new job. But no one here seems like they want me in the corporate office. Is it that bad? Have I really been that difficult to deal with?" he asked. The answer was "Yes, you have." I could feel his hurt over the phone.

"Hal, you can fix this. You have the ability and now you have the reason to make the changes you need to make," I said. We agreed that our goal would be a party. Not a party that we threw for *him* but a party that we would throw every day in the lives of his *employees*. Hal committed himself to becoming more expressive and especially nurturing to those around him. One goal, in particular, was that he would do everything he could to celebrate his team and see that his people earned promotions, raises, bonuses, and opportunities. Instead of thinking about *his* career, he was going to take steps to nurture the careers of those around him.

He made the same commitment to his family. Hal was going to love his wife in an unselfish way, and he was going to praise his boys daily for the things they did that were positive. He was a man on a mission, and that mission was his personal growth.

I visited Hal a few weeks ago. He is now global CFO for Agate, and he sits next door to Mike Steele and the chairman of the board, Tom Woolford. The men that worked directly under Hal in Austin came to Dallas with him. He became a much more nurturing man, and when he was offered the position as CFO, they threw a party for him because *he* had learned to celebrate *them*. Hal is more outgoing, friendly, and nurturing today than he could have ever imagined, and his life is richer for it. Being nurturing is not about being soft or touchy-feely. It is about caring for others and learning how to express it.

Are You an Iceberg?

Check any of the following symptoms that occur and add up the total.

- [ ] People can and should solve their own problems.
- [ ] I generally screen calls, and if it's important enough, I can return the call later.
- [ ] Others would say I'm not the most affectionate person.
- [ ] I don't compliment people as much as others do.
- [ ] I am more closed off when around people I'm not as comfortable with.
- [ ] Showing nurturing behaviors makes me feel awkward, even with people close to me.

☐ I rarely stop to think of something I can do for someone else.

☐ I don't usually make a point to greet people, especially strangers.

☐ It's not unusual for people to ask me what I'm thinking because I can be hard to read.

☐ It's not my responsibility to help others feel good about themselves.

Iceberg Tendencies?

Mark your total below.

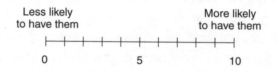

So I'm an Iceberg—Help Me!

A quote from Molière comes to mind that captures the essence of this: "It is not only for what we do that we are held responsible, but also for what we do not do." A friend of mine confessed to me recently that he felt alone. He said that deep down he cared about people but just didn't connect with them and didn't take the time to show them how much he cared.

Quite often this constraint shows up even more in our outer circle of acquaintances. Some of you may demonstrate several nurturing behaviors with people you are close to, likely because you feel safer with them. On the other hand, you may appear more closed off or serious around others you don't know as well. You may have a warmth and expressiveness somewhere inside, but you need to show that side to more people.

Emotional connection is a good concept to keep in mind. Stop and think for a moment about your two closest friends from your entire life. I would speculate that those are friends with whom you established an emotional connection. In fact, you probably have had other friends whom you spent even more time with.

So let's make sure to look for opportunities to capture the emotion of those around us. Invest in their emotional bank accounts in order to form a lasting relationship that will weather the storms of life.

Specific TrAction Steps

Here are some sample action steps you can take to start getting traction—today! Once you read all of the constraint chapters, if this is determined to be one of your killer constraints, then steps like these will be part of your TrAction Plan (to be built in chapter 15).

• Every day I will not go to sleep until I have done at least one of the following: (1) sent an encouraging e-mail, (2) called to affirm someone, or (3) given someone a compliment. This will help me build up my emotional bank accounts with people.

• I will start engaging people when I encounter them. Stopping what I am doing, I will enthusiastically greet them with a smile. Even if I am in the middle of a task, I can converse for a couple of minutes and then politely let the person know I need to get back to my responsibilities.

• I will start finding out more about the people I spend time with, saying something like: "I may have given you the impression that I didn't value you enough, so can you help hold me accountable to tending to our relationship better?" I will intentionally ask deeper questions to discover what is important to people, such as "How is your family?" or "What has been on your mind lately?" Also, I will be vulnerable so that they can get to know the real me.

How Can I Deal with an Iceberg?

To effectively deal with someone like this, it is always important to make sure the person feels validated. Even the extreme of each constraint contains some positives, so make sure you communicate the positives also. Here are some potential strengths to validate: Not getting caught up in unnecessary emotion, Not getting lost in relationships over other priorities.

• If you are having a hard time seeing a warmer side, instead of waiting and hoping, it may be better to ask specific questions such as "Do you like what I expressed?" or "I'm having a hard time reading you—can you tell me more about what you like about this?" Have realistic expectations because this person may not shift his or her behavior drastically.

• Because Icebergs are emotionally tough, it is all right to say things more directly. If you need affirmation from them, let them know, and be specific if necessary. If their response isn't enough, ask again, and be more specific. You can be fairly direct with them, but they will need specific behaviors that they can do. Help them understand that it would benefit them to add this emotional component and that it will likely help their relationships and their productivity. It is possible they could react by thinking or saying that you are "needy," so be ready to objectively respond that it isn't about you and that it might be a good idea for them to get additional opinions. Lastly, don't get dismayed when they don't meet your expectations the next time the same situation comes up. They may not see even a glaring need at times, so be patient with them as they develop this ability.

10 *Killer Constraint #6:* Flatliners (Low Passion, Vision, or Drive)

Several months ago, I got a call from David, a longtime friend. As we were finishing up our conversation, he asked if I would take his son to lunch one day and talk with him about his future. David shared that Michael had been struggling with finding a career and deciding what to do with his life. It had been years since we had last visited together, and I thought it would be great to see him again.

We met at a local restaurant, and like all growing, college-age men, Michael ordered everything on the menu. Quantity is what seems to matter most when you are that age, and it was good to see him enjoying his meal. As we visited he shared information about the courses he had been taking and how he wasn't really excited about any of them. Thus far in his course work, he had enough classes to be a senior, but they were spread out all over the board and in no specific major, so he wasn't anywhere close to graduating. In fact, he was already in his fifth year and still short another year's worth of courses to graduate.

"So how are your classes going?" I asked.

"Well, I dropped a few of them this semester because I got behind and didn't feel like they would help me toward graduation after I looked at what I needed," he responded. When I asked, "How many hours were you taking, and what did you drop?" his response floored me. "I was taking fifteen hours, but I'm only taking three now. I figured I didn't need the rest of them if I decide to change majors again."

I couldn't believe it. He had dropped twelve hours *in one semester*—after signing up and paying for courses that he hadn't even checked to make sure would count toward his major in the first place! Why would you sign up for something that you aren't going to finish, then pay for it, and then drop it?

The answer to that one was easy. Someone else was paying for it.

Michael's parents are good people. They earn their money the old-fashioned way—they work for it. David has a good job, but it requires a lot of travel and long hours. David's wife also works, and she carries the extra burden that comes with having a husband away two nights a week.

"Michael, when did you get up this morning?" I asked.

"Oh, man, I stayed out too late last night and didn't get up early." . He grinned.

"Well, I stayed up late, too, but what time did you get up?"

"A little before I was supposed to meet you for lunch."

Let's see if I have this right. He stayed up late, he doesn't have a job other than school, he goes to class only three hours per week, and he didn't get up until we were meeting for lunch. Tough life. At the least I appreciated his honesty.

"Michael, did you know I had a heart attack a few years ago?"

"Yeah, I had heard that. Are you all right now?" he asked.

"Yes, but I have cardiovascular disease and have had three surgeries since then. I eat right and work out and am in great shape now that we have it under control," I replied.

"That's good," he said.

We finished our meals, and soon, the discussion turned to the topic he wanted to talk about—his career.

"I need to find something that will let me work the hours I want and still make good money. I like not having too much pressure, and I want to have some time to spend with my friends. I'm not sure what I want to do, but that's the kind of job I'm looking for," he said. "What do you think I ought to be doing for a career?"

He couldn't have handed me a better opportunity.

I leaned over and said, "Michael, you know our business is doing well, don't you?"

"Sure."

"Well, I have a job for you, but you might not like it. It's not hard for the first few years, and in fact, you can do pretty much whatever you want. Then it will get harder."

He sat up straight, his eyes lighting up. "Wow—sounds good to me. What is it?"

I leaned over, getting so close he probably thought I was going to kiss him. "I think you ought to consider being this: a *donor.* In a few years, I could use a new heart, and you aren't doing squat with the healthy one that you have, so I thought I might go ahead and pay you for yours now. And then later, when I need it, I could collect on it. You're wasting your life, and I'm not, so it seems only right that I would be able to have the opportunity to finish the important projects that I've been working on. What do you say? Do we have a deal?"

Michael's jaw dropped, and he looked at me like I had just kicked his dog. Yes, it was the cold, hard truth. But it was the truth. I leaned over again and took his face in both of my hands.

I said, "Child, you are worthless with what you are doing with yourself. Get off your butt and do something with the talents you have. And by the way, don't call me for lunch unless you are going to class and have something to show for it. You have extraordinary potential, but every day you waste is an insult to the gifts you were given. Finish school and do something with your life—or take me up on my deal."

I kissed his forehead right there in the restaurant, got up and hugged him, and we walked out.

Many months passed, and then he called. Michael was graduating and had some solid interviews in line for jobs. He ended up taking a good position with a reputable company and is doing well today.

He laughs now when he tells the story to others, but he had gotten the point.

Perhaps it came from my granddad—I'm not sure. It's difficult for me to understand people who don't try to do something with the life they've been given. Over the years I've watched a friend who is severely mentally challenged get up every day and go to a job that is, at best, low paying—yet he always seems to have a great day. To listen to him talk about helping people with their groceries and to know his customers and their children by name, you would think that he is changing the world. Actually, he *is* changing the world. Then I see so many others who have been given so much yet do so little. Too often it takes a crisis or life-threatening situation before Flatliners are jolted into the realization that time is fleeting and life is too precious to waste.

Betsy Nagelsen and Billie Jean King

Betsy Nagelsen (mentioned back in chapter 2) had just joined the pro ranks of tennis at nineteen, which at that time was young for a tennis pro, and Billie Jean King, the tennis legend and icon, was finishing out her incredible career. She was still ranked at the top and had dominated the sport for several years. It was 1975, and Billie Jean had invited Betsy to travel with her and train with some of the top-ranked players in the world.

Betsy was thrilled. She was hitting with the top contenders—the opportunity of a lifetime. Once during the tour Billie came to her room and asked Betsy a direct question.

"Do you want to be the best?"

Of course any young kid is going to say yes, and that is what Betsy said.

"Yeah, but do you *really* want to win?"

"Sure I do."

"How bad do you want it?" Billie almost shouted.

"Real bad," Betsy responded somewhat weakly.

"Do you want it more than *anything?* Do you *really* want it? Do you want it worse than *anything else* in the whole world? Do you want it more than anything you can *think* of? Are you ready to sacrifice *everything you have* to win?"

By now Betsy was beginning to wonder, "Wow...do I really want it *that bad?*" But still she said, "Sure, I want it," even though inside she saw the difference between Billie Jean and herself. She laughs today that she remembers that being one pep talk that left her halfway depressed.

That day Betsy saw something that few others ever get to see. She saw passion in its purest form. Winning meant more to Billie Jean than it did to almost anyone else in the world of women's tennis. During this time Billie was indomitable. No one could beat her. She seemed driven beyond her abilities, and yet she kept on winning. She inspired women around her to see themselves as having the ability to be truly great in sports and that they were worth more than the going rate for women's sports at that time. Billie Jean was on fire, and the world was watching as she lit up the world stage of tennis.

In 1973 an estimated fifty million viewers were glued to their TV sets during prime time when the famous "Battle of the Sexes" match settled the age-old question: are women good enough to compete with men? Few people thought Billie Jean had a chance, including many of her own closest friends. But Bobby Riggs had challenged her, and if women were to ever be taken seriously, she *had* to win. Billie Jean King beat Bobby Riggs in three straight sets.

It would be years later that Betsy would look back and understand the power of passion. Billie Jean wasn't just about winning her matches. She was inspiring a nation of women and opening doors for them in the world of professional sports.

When a love to compete is combined with a joy in simply being in the present, life is full of pleasure. Passion and drive are unbeatable traits. If you want to go to the top, you have to have them. Passion should be like a fire burning inside you. Sometimes it's just a warm feeling that you know is there. At other times that fire should be a roaring furnace that drives you beyond your own abilities and into "the zone" of wherever you are truly wanting to go. Passion and drive are perhaps the two greatest determinants of success in life.

Remember, if you aren't on fire about something, the world is a cold place to be.

Don't Wait

I would be remiss if I didn't tell you something else that our research has shown us. Passion and drive are learned behavioral traits. Children can be taught passion and drive that will cause them to excel. However, it is extremely difficult to put passion and drive into an adult's life once they are past about thirty years of age.

If you have ever hired someone, you know that they either come to work ready and committed, or they come to work and barely get anything done. I agree with the response from that great football coach Lou Holtz when he was asked, "Coach, how do you get such motivated players?" Lou said, "It's not hard to have a fully motivated team. I get rid of the ones that aren't motivated."

Motivation, drive, passion, and desire for success are developed during the early life of a person. You can see it on the field when a child is playing soccer or in the classroom when he or she is doing a lab experiment. It is readily spotted when a child is practicing a music lesson, or painting, or doing anything that person is fervent about.

Passion in a child is a tiny flame that can be quenched early on or fanned by someone with vision—someone who looks past what *is* to what *could be*.

Everyone Needs a Mrs. Finnell

The sixth grade was hard for me. The math was getting tougher, and I was looking at failing if drastic measures weren't taken. Cheating didn't seem that drastic, especially since I had two buddies that felt the same way. I had been cheating all year.

Every few days we had math homework. The day our homework was due Mrs. Finnell would ask us to exchange papers with a class-mate, and we would grade each other's papers as she called out the answers. After passing our papers back to the owner, we would call out our grade so she could record it in the grade book. Two of my friends came to the realization that we could exchange our papers among the three of us, and she wouldn't figure out that we were "fix-ing" our grades. I might change papers with Bobby one day and the next day with Tommy. We would leave the answers blank, and then as she called out the answers we would fill them in for each other. Of course it was important that we didn't get *too* good a grade, so we would be sure that occasionally we missed some answers. Because we were so smart, we had been getting away with this all year long.

One day the world stopped.

We had exchanged our papers, and Mrs. Finnell was getting ready to call out the answers. But this time she did something different. She got out of her chair and walked over to Bobby and asked for the paper that he had in his hand. Then she walked over to Tommy and asked for his paper as well. Next, she turned toward me and asked for my paper also. Then she sat back down and called out the answers as she always did. We sat there at our empty desks waiting. And waiting. This defi-nitely spelled trouble for the three of us. We were probably going to die.

That afternoon as soon as school was out, I raced home on my bike and waited by the phone. I knew she would call and tell my mother, and I would get a beating. I was ready. When she called I was going to try to sound like my dad and tell her I knew and that I would take care of it. Then I would go on about my business like nothing had ever happened because I would still be alive.

The phone never rang. I waited there for hours. Finally supper came, and still no call. Then bedtime came—*and still she had not called.* How would I ever answer the phone if she called after bed-time? But it didn't ring.

The next day nothing happened at school. No one talked to us about it, and Mrs. Finnell didn't say a word. I raced home again and waited for the call, but it didn't come. The following day was the same.

Then Friday came, and I thought I was going to make it. I always pitched at softball during recess. That day I was pitching, and during the game Mrs. Finnell walked toward the field. I was hoping she was coming to play ball with us. She was the only woman I ever saw who could slide into second base with a dress on and make it look natural. But she didn't come to play.

She stopped at the baseline and motioned for me to come over. I walked toward her and wondered at the same time where I could go hide. When I got to her, she looked at me and said, "Flip, you know I have been watching you all this year, don't you?"

"Yes, ma'am" was all I could choke out.

"I want you to know that I think that someday you are going to be a great baseball player," she said. And then she walked away. I stood there. I was so embarrassed and ashamed of what I had done. I had let her down. I had cheated on the lady who thought I was going to be a great baseball player. I felt like a bum. Yet despite everything, she saw something in me that she set in motion that day.

Years later I was in a meeting with some of the leadership of the Texas Rangers baseball team and needed to take a break. We had been going over some pretty intense information, and after a few hours of sitting, I got up and walked out to the hallway. Shortly after, Reid Nichols walked out behind me. Reid was in charge of player development for the team and is well known for his coach's heart and enthusiasm. He stopped me in the hall and asked if I was all right. I nodded.

He gave me an "I'm not buying it" look. "You're feeling something. What's going on?"

"Reid, I was thinking about where we are, and what we are doing, and I was thinking about Mrs. Finnell."

"*Who* is Mrs. Finnell?"

"She was my sixth-grade teacher. Reid, do you know where we are?"

"Sure I do. It's where I work," he responded.

"Yes it is. We are standing in Texas Stadium going through the data on several of your players to see what we can do to get them ready for the next level. And Mrs. Finnell knew I would be here. Reid, *she saw me here.*"

I told Reid the story. I also let him know that I was available as a free agent if he saw a fit. By the way I'm still available if anyone reading this has an opening for a pretty good left-handed pitcher.

I come highly recommended by Mrs. Finnell.

Are You a Flatliner?

Check any of the following symptoms that occur and add up the total.

- ☐ People constantly tell me I'm very laid back.
- ☐ At work it helps me to have someone check in with me and help set deadlines.
- ☐ I seem to work better when there is pressure to get something done. I am not as intense at the beginning of a project.
- ☐ I think that people who work really hard miss the point of life.
- ☐ I'm not considered for promotions very often.
- ☐ It is very important to stop and smell the roses.
- ☐ I would not be described as an intense, highly driven person.
- ☐ If called upon, I can deliver, but I rarely offer my services on my own initiative.
- ☐ I use work time to do a lot of personal business.
- ☐ I don't have a strong picture of what I can do and where I am headed.

Flatliner Tendencies?

Mark your total below.

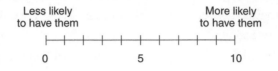

So I'm a Flatliner—Help Me!

Mark Twain once said, "The secret of success is making your vocation your vacation."

So what do you want to be when you grow up? Regardless of your age you probably haven't decided. I'm not sure I have either.

Research shows that some people have an innate intensity that allows them to, at least for a season, tackle almost any task with a sense of urgency. But most people aren't like that, and here is my challenge to those people: find a job you truly enjoy—one in which you feel equipped to succeed. Easier said than done, of course, but this reality cannot be ignored. The truth is that all jobs have parts that you won't enjoy, so be realistic. But look for that one aspect of the job that you can really pour yourself into, the part that at the end of a hard day you can smile about.

The difficult aspect of this constraint is the perception it gives. Picture an intense, task-oriented person working closely with someone who is more easygoing. It's a recipe for disaster, with the driven person frequently making statements such as "Let's keep moving. What are we each committing to? What are the assignments?" and the laid-back person saying, "Can you just relax? I want to make sure everyone is heard. Let's explore that line of thinking for a while. If we don't get everything done in an hour, that's fine."

The truth is that if you keep doing what you are doing, you'll keep getting what you are getting. So if you are tired of getting frustrated with people who are really task oriented, then what can you do differently to communicate a sense of urgency? If you're tired of being passed over for promotions, what feedback could you solicit to understand why? If you miss a deadline but there's always a reason, then commit to finishing early next time.

Want to know a behavior that people really respect and are drawn to? It's having passion. Look for some tasks you can get excited about and get some feedback about your productivity—then deliver early.

Specific TrAction Steps

Here are some sample action steps you can take to start getting traction—today! Once you read all of the constraint chapters, if this is determined to be one of your killer constraints, then steps like these will be part of your TrAction Plan (to be built in chapter 15).

• To become more disciplined I will stop rewarding myself before I have earned a break. I will organize my to-do list and prioritize the top several items. And I will place a small reward after each one, such as taking a five-minute break, getting a drink, going on a short walk. [For larger tasks, break them up into smaller ones.] If possible I will have someone check on my progress more frequently until I can become self-managing.

• I will start being early instead of late. Avoiding excuses, if I miss a deadline I will make a point to express, "I apologize for giving you the impression that I didn't take the task seriously enough. I look forward to proving myself next time." And if I sense that I might miss a deadline, I will update the team with the current status and ask, "Does anyone have any ideas about what I could do differently to speed up the process?"

• I will start looking for my passion in life by really examining my job/career choice to make sure that it is personally rewarding. I am more likely to be successful if I align my personal values with a job that I am reasonably passionate about.

How Can I Deal with a Flatliner?

To effectively deal with someone like this, it is always important to make sure the person feels validated. Even the extreme of each constraint contains some positives, so make sure you communicate the positives also. Here are some potential strengths to validate: Easygoing, Relaxed.

• To motivate Flatliners, be sure to break up tasks into small, measurable chunks and celebrate accomplishments and potentially offer rewards as an incentive. Help them feel a sense of success, and hopefully they will want to experience that feeling more often.

• Have realistic expectations about Flatliners taking frequent initiative. They aren't wired to do that, so it would be better to put them in positions that require less initiative and have more explicit expectations. Provide reasonable guidelines for their productivity and be patient while attempting to spark their intensity.

11 *Killer Constraint #7:*
Bulldozers (Overly Dominant)

Dominant people tend to run things. That's not a problem unless they do so at the expense of the contributions of others.

I was working with a Texas school district on a process to help them raise their students' test scores (as well as the performance of their educators). That is how I met the superintendent, "Teresa."

The hills were turning to beautiful orange and soft browns as the sun set behind them. The golf course in front of us was perfectly cared for, and the creek that ran through the retreat setting was surprisingly cold for Texas. The whole atmosphere was perfect. As we were sitting down to start the discussion, Teresa blurted out, "I'm in a hurry and don't want to waste time with pleasantries, so who has the agenda?"

I sat quietly, watching with interest.

"I know what I want, and I know how it needs to be done. So let's skip the debate about how this program ought to move forward," she said next.

One of my team said, "We really need to go over the information together. I'd like to share with you what we have done in several hundred other districts to accomplish the goals you are after. We have a lot of experience in schools just like yours and can save you considerable money and heartache—with just a few simple changes."

"That is all well and good, but I still know what I want. So let's dispense with that part of the discussion," she responded.

The meeting took about twenty minutes, as Teresa ran through her agenda and asked several very pointed questions of her staff. They brought up some things that she needed to look at, which she quickly dismissed without further discussion. She was a bottom-line kind of lady, and her interest was in her agenda. As soon as she was finished with her business, she left.

We continued discussing some of the issues that had been raised, and it was clear that her staff members were uncomfortable. Finally one of them turned to me and said, "Flip, I apologize for how that came off. She is under a lot of pressure, and there is a lot riding on what your team is doing with us." I nodded in understanding. My team is frequently brought into situations during times of transition and great pressure.

But pressure is no excuse for bad behavior.

We were the experts in implementing our processes and knew better than she how to help her achieve her goals. But she would never know that unless she took time to hear us.

I asked her staff a question: "Wouldn't it make sense if you let us walk you through this process so that you aren't wasting money and ending up with something that none of us are happy about?"

We were surprised when they agreed, and we continued the discussion in that vein. Time flew by, and we were all pleased with the savings they would make and, more important, with the outcomes, which would result in more students being successful.

A few days later Teresa called and informed us of her plans and how we were to move forward. I asked if she had reviewed the work her staff had done, and she responded, "No, I haven't had time. I know how I want it done, so let's agree that will be how we move forward." I wasn't surprised, but I was certainly disappointed.

Months later I called one of the senior people in her group and found out that he had taken some sick days. I called him at home to see if we could help in any way and to let him know we were thinking of him. "What's the problem?" I politely asked, not wanting to intrude too much. "I have bleeding ulcers and have developed irritable bowel syndrome. I've been ordered to stay home in bed for two weeks." Again I wasn't surprised. The source of much of the stress they were under was clear, and it wasn't pretty.

A few months later I was back with Teresa and her team, going over the personal-growth data that we had gathered on each senior person. The goal was to help them accelerate their performance professionally as well as personally. Everyone was excited about getting his or her information, but as soon as it was passed out, Teresa stood up. She announced that she had a luncheon she didn't want to miss and that she would be back in a couple of hours. Everyone else began going through the data and working enthusiastically in teams. Teresa never came back that day.

I called her a week later and offered to come to her office (three hours away) and meet with her personally to go over her data. It was then that she told me her agenda. "I intend them to go through this process, but I don't have time for personal growth. I'm paying you to improve *them,* and that's what I'm looking for."

Remember what we discussed earlier about no team being able to rise above the constraints of its leader? Within the next few months, most of her team began aggressively pursuing other jobs.

And a year later?

Well, let's say that Teresa "retired" from her position. She is now serving as a consultant for other districts. Sad, but true.

The Crush of the Bulldozer

Overly dominant people are tough. They are tough to be around, and they are tough to deal with. Sadly, they usually think they are the answer and final word regarding anything. They argue with people, and they run over people who don't bend like they want. In marriages they are very difficult to deal with, and only the strong or the foolish survive those experiences.

They may be right about 90 percent of their points, but they are 100 percent *wrong* in the way they deal with people. And, to top it off, they are bullies. They lose relationships and employees easily because they don't care about what they do to them.

A balanced dominance is the mark of a good leader. You have to have people who will make things happen. I know because I am a take-charge type of person. I also know what happens when dominance gets too high. Thankfully I have several people who, over the years, have gotten in my face and told me when I was wrong—not necessarily wrong about a point, but certainly wrong about not listening and being so impatient to move forward. The people who live on the high side of dominance are the ones who bulldoze their way through life.

Bulldozers: Short on Humility and Perspective

One evening my wife and I were visiting with a small group of friends that included Mark and Betsy McCormack; newscaster Paula Zahn and her husband, Richard; Ray Cave (the former managing editor of *Time*); Howard and Janet Katz (Howard was past president of ABC Sports and is now head of NFL films); and Nando Parrado, whose harrowing story of survival in the snowbound Andes was told in the bestselling book *Alive!* Needless to say Susan and I were the least renowned of the group but probably the most pleased with the evening.

Nando, in his quiet and simple way, gave us his personal version of the famous 1972 plane crash in the Andes Mountains that killed his mother and sister, along with many members of his rugby team and their families. Initially unconscious for three days, Nando awoke to discover that only he and fifteen of his teammates had survived the tragedy and that the most horrific aspects of his experience were still ahead. After seventy-two days of battling subzero temperatures, starvation, and avalanches with no supplies or medical attention, the group finally realized they were waiting for a rescue that would never come. Without a clue as to where they were, it was decided that twenty-three-year-old Nando would lead a three-man expedition over forty-five miles of frozen mountain wilderness to reach Chile and bring back help. His account of the obstacles and his determination to reach his grief-stricken father—or perish trying—ranks as one of the most dramatic survival stories of our time.

After Nando had finished sharing his amazing story, we sat down for dinner. I was reflecting on the day, struck by the clear contrast of his humble telling of a truly heroic event with an earlier meeting Betsy and I had with a businessman who had talked nonstop about himself the entire meeting. Regaling us with all the details of his accomplishments and his importance, the businessman monopolized our meeting with information regarding a business deal that he was currently putting together. Since he had not once taken the time to inquire about anyone else in the meeting, he never knew he was in the presence of several others whose accomplishments far exceeded his. Nonetheless, we sat quietly while he bragged of his feats without letting anyone else get a word in edgewise. Overall our meeting was a long and painful event.

I thought about the amazing contrasts in people. Nando's life was one of quiet excellence and commitment, while the other man's was one of arrogance and self-importance. Certainly there was no question as to which man understood what true leadership was.

Are You a Bulldozer?

Check any of the following symptoms that occur and add up the total.

- ☐ I often finish other people's sentences.
- ☐ When I disagree with others, it's okay to interrupt to correct them.
- ☐ I am comfortable leading a large group of people by actively taking charge.

☐ Being strong willed enables me to accomplish more than others.

☐ I am comfortable with heated discussions.

☐ When others are talking, I am already thinking of what to say next and looking for an opportunity to win them to my way of thinking.

☐ I can be pushy and maybe even hardheaded, but I'm usually right.

☐ If I'm in charge I don't like people stepping on my toes—people should stick to their role.

☐ People have said I'm stubborn, but I just have strong opinions.

☐ Weaker people shouldn't be in charge of things.

Bulldozer Tendencies?

Mark your total below.

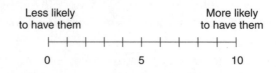

So I'm a Bulldozer—Help Me!

You might be thinking: Is this really that big of a constraint? What's wrong with me being in charge—doesn't someone have to be? What if people like who I am, including the fact that I'm more assertive? Could it be that I'm just a great leader? If I got input from everybody, wouldn't I waste a lot of time? Do I really need to get votes from everyone if I already know the best option?

Did you notice what all of the above questions have in common? They're all about you. And when it comes to this constraint, that may be the greatest lesson to take home: it's not about you.

The reality is that people usually don't write in big bold letters that we've been running over them. They may speak by moving on to another opportunity, and there may be hurt that was never expressed. I would venture that most of the people whom you've had heated discussions with or whom you have perceived as pushy had this in common: being similar to you!

But let's remember that the goal isn't to become passive. The goal is to keep the strengths of being strong willed while also minimizing the damage. Instead of the leader that builds followers, be the leader that builds other leaders!

Specific TrAction Steps

Here are some sample action steps you can take to start getting traction—today! Once you read all of the constraint chapters, if this is determined to be one of your killer constraints, then steps like these will be part of your TrAction Plan (to be built in chapter 15).

• I will start taking a step back in group interactions at times. If I have an opinion, I will hold my thought and see if anyone else steps up to express a similar perspective. Instead of clarifying my position, I will focus on asking more reserved people what their thoughts are, being willing to say things such as "No, you go ahead, I insist." I will avoid interrupting other people or finishing their sentences. [Designate a specific person to watch you and hold you accountable during a few interactions.]

• I will start checking in more during conversations by asking, "Am I answering your question?" or "Am I giving you the impression that I am really listening?" or "Do you feel strongly about this? Tell me more." Communication is more than just tag-team talking, so I will better engage the people I have discussions with.

• I will start getting more agreement from those around me. To avoid being perceived as pushy, I will become further aware of my tendency to take charge and will intentionally step back and observe more. I will avoid seeing a decision as black or white and will try to better understand how others are feeling about the decision, as opposed to just thinking about the facts.

• I will start getting more feedback on how I am perceived by others. For example, at the end of a meeting I could ask someone, "Did I listen well and participate proportionally?" Or I could ask someone whom I work closely with, "Do you feel like I'm overcontrolling at times? Do I ever micromanage you?" [Have someone give you feedback once a week on a specific question like one of these.]

How Can I Deal with a Bulldozer?

To effectively deal with someone like this, it is always important to make sure the person feels validated. Even the extreme of each constraint contains some positives, so make sure you communicate the positives also. Here are some potential strengths to validate: Decisive, Strong willed, Assertive, Leadership ability.

• Be sure to ask questions about what Bulldozers think and how they feel. Say things such as "Your opinion is really important to me—tell me more" to help reinforce that you value their perspective. If you are feeling pushed on or run over, it is appropriate to say that you aren't feeling heard. Let them know that you want to hear them but that you want the same courtesy in return.

• Provide clear guidelines when appropriate for interactions with Bulldozers. For example, before a meeting you might clarify, "We have an hour together, and here are the topics we really need to cover...." This will make it clear who is running the meeting and help him or her understand if you need to take the reins.

12 *Killer Constraint #8:*
Turtles (Resistant to Change)

A Tale of Two Wives

I know two couples who have made differing choices about their lives. One couple, Mike and Valerie Smith, has raised three bright, artistically gifted children. My wife and I have been part of their lives over the last few years as they have chosen to walk through some challenging times. One day Mike and Valerie decided they wanted to leave their comfortable careers and move to another country to work with a relief program.

They discussed it with the rest of the family, and although there were a lot of questions and uncertainties to work through, the decision was finally made to go. The family packed up their modest belongings and moved five thousand miles away from family and friends to begin a new life in a country with a different language and very different customs. We stayed in touch with them because we were quite interested in the work they were doing as well as the people they were working with.

On our first visit to see them overseas, we noticed that Valerie never left the house. We also noticed that she didn't drive, so the only time she was able to go anywhere was when Mike took her out for errands. Her life was centered around her family, which of course is a good thing if it is not hindering other areas that need some attention. When the topic came up, you could tell Valerie felt quite comfortable focusing all her energies at home.

The problem was that Mike couldn't do his community-based work effectively without her becoming a more outgoing person. His work really did require that Valerie be part of it in a more active way. When this was discussed you could see her visible resistance to it. It wasn't that Valerie wasn't supportive of Mike's mission or that she didn't love people or see the need to be more involved in the community. In fact, Valerie had wanted to serve in this way since she was a child, and she had already worked with Mike in other countries.

It all boiled down to one thing—a personal constraint. Valerie didn't like change. The thought of meeting new people, and hosting them in her home, and trying to make small talk in another language was more than she wanted to take on. It was easier to stay in her home and learn to be a gourmet cook—which she did very well. But that didn't help Mike with his work, which was what she had committed to him before they left the States. Mike's life expanded in the new community as he met more and more people, while Valerie continued to live a very "small" life wrapped around her kitchen and children.

It was obvious to us that Valerie struggled with change and that she was afraid of making mistakes in public, using the wrong words in a new language or making some cultural misstep. It wasn't about her being selfish or aloof—she cared deeply for people—she was just fearful of making mistakes, and it was much easier to stay at home and do what she knew how to do rather than venture into unknown territory.

Her Turtle ways showed up in many areas of her life. She wasn't learning how to drive a stick-shift car or get familiar with the area. She was meeting only a few people in the community. She didn't invite new people over, and she rarely went outside her home. But she needed to do all of those things if she was going to participate in the life they had moved into together.

Doug and Sandy

Our other friends had married while in college. Doug had wanted to be a teacher, and Sandy had wanted to teach also, but only until they had children. She had grown up in a small, close-knit family, and Doug had lived in a small town until he left for college. They were a perfect match.

When they talked about their future, they both wanted the same things. Doug wanted a job with meaning, and Sandy wanted a family. They both wanted to be together and do something that made a difference. When Doug finished school he started interviewing for a teaching job but couldn't get one in their hometown area. He needed work, so he started looking at other things that would help him take care of his young family. A friend mentioned an open sales position, and even though he had no experience in sales, he needed a job, so he took it.

After the first year Doug found he had a real aptitude for his new line of work. He enjoyed working with customers, and he excelled in the sales job. The next year Doug continued to do well, and that allowed them to actually have a real vacation. Life was looking good. Sandy had some concerns about the time Doug was spending at work, but she was busy with the children. Doug made every game and rehearsal he could, and he bragged for hours about his kids and his wife. There was no question that they loved each other very much.

With success comes opportunity, and that is what happened for Doug and Sandy. Doug received a promotion offer, and after much discussion with Sandy, he accepted it. Both of them knew that this new job meant more work and some travel, but they felt they could make the adjustments. They also had to move to another city. Sandy didn't like the idea of moving away, but she knew that there was only so much opportunity for someone in a small town. Doug even talked about trying to get a teaching job again if that was what they each felt was right. But that wouldn't have allowed them to do the things they wanted for their kids, and besides, Doug really seemed gifted at what he was doing. He was the top performer in a midsize company, and the future looked great for him.

But as the years passed, Doug's extra responsibilities and Sandy's reaction started causing trouble in their relationship. Sandy was having a hard time with the changes. Doug didn't have an eight-to-five job, and it wouldn't have fit his passion for life if he had. In many ways he was outgrowing her. Doug's world was expanding, while Sandy's was shrinking. She was involved with the children to the extent that she had no other outside activities. Even the expression on her face belied a general unhappiness with her life.

They were making more money than they had ever imagined, which was fine with Sandy, but she wasn't happy.

Then Doug got an opportunity to join another firm in a position that required international travel. Sandy didn't like what was happening. To her each new opportunity meant only that she had to "change and sacrifice more."

One day Doug finally asked Sandy, "Are you happy for me and the things I am doing, or are you going to resent me the rest of my life?" Sandy had a question for him, too: "I didn't marry you with the idea that you were going to be traveling the world. I thought I was marrying a teacher who would never leave town. Why isn't that enough for you?"

You could see where this conflict was headed. Sandy was faced with the same issue that Valerie had to deal with: change. Life isn't what you think it's going to be—life is what it becomes. Part of it stems from choices we make, but part of our life is simply an unfolding adventure that we must choose to reject or adapt to as it presents itself to us. Whether we like it or not, we are touched and influenced by others and what happens to them. This is a great deal of what marriage is all about.

The question is this: are we able to change to accommodate the things that come into our life? Certainly we should have a say in what goes on in a marriage or, for that matter, any relationship. But are we open to new opportunities even if they were not in the original "plan" we thought we signed up for?

How would Sandy have felt if Doug had become a teacher in a small town (which I think might be a really good thing), only to find that he was incredibly unhappy in that role? What happens if he begins to feel that he has never fulfilled his own dreams? No matter what direction we take, there are always alternatives with pros and cons to each different outcome. I think the goal is to be able to respond to what comes up and deal with it with the best attitude that we can muster.

The two couples handled their situations differently. Overseas, Valerie made a choice. A good friend had challenged her to look at what she *wasn't* doing to further the work that they were involved in. Since she was a "processor" who turns over information and thinks through it, her friend's feedback sank in and she made a decision. One morning she got up and said, "Mike, teach me how to drive the stick shift so you don't have to drive me everywhere I need to go." She ultimately decided to change, even though it was scary for her. She is still changing. We visited Mike and Valerie in their home again recently, and we had a ball. She is still the best cook around, but she has also learned a new language, become very active in the community, and is even showing her artwork in local civic events. The transformation has been beautiful, and you can see the pride on her husband's face as he shares about her latest meetings and exploits. Valerie has become a tremendous role model for those around her in the process, and her enthusiasm for life is contagious. Mike and Valerie have become a great team.

Sandy still struggles, even though Doug has made it clear he will do anything he can to help her feel more complete. Their children are almost grown, and Sandy recently said, "I don't have to let go of my feelings. This is not what I signed up for, and I don't have to like it." Well, that's true. But people grow and change, and when others won't accept or try to work with those changes, something usually breaks.

What could Sandy do to make her situation better? One thing would be to help Doug set boundaries around his schedule. Together, they could mark off the things that should be kept "sacred" and are not up for grabs when someone else has a need. Sandy could also plan to accompany him on some business trips so that they could have time together even if it's not the entire time. In addition, Sandy has to build a life that she is happy with. This could be as simple as devoting more time to friends along with finding activities that are meaningful to her. The bottom line is that she is responsible for her own actions and that includes making her own life more acceptable to her. Again, a great part of that is dealing with her own attitude and making the changes that give her a deeper sense of purpose, especially as the children are leaving home.

Flopping His Way to Success

If Dick Fosbury had listened to just about anybody—including, at times, himself—he never would have been standing in that warm Mexico City sunlight on October 20, 1968, staring at a high-jump bar perched 2.24 meters (that's 7 feet 4.25 inches) above the ground.

Fosbury was arguably the least athletic competitor at the Mexico City Olympics in any sport. Scrawny physique, average speed, a modest vertical jump. His only competitive advantage came from his unique jumping style, an ungainly backward flop that appeared to risk a broken neck on every attempt. Every other jumper straddled the bar, and Fosbury's new approach enraged sports purists and horrified mothers of adolescent high jumpers around the world.

Virtually all track-and-field folks begrudged Fosbury his success. They viewed him as an aberration and his increasing success as a passing streak of luck. Every coach he worked with urged him to abandon the weird technique that flouted every bit of conventional wisdom about his event. Even though he had won a national high-school championship with his method, his coach at Oregon State pushed him to master the straddle—and Fosbury agreed.

But during practices Fosbury continued to experiment with the flop, and halfway through college his coach decided to film Fosbury's misadventures—hoping to clearly demonstrate why it was an inferior method. Instead the pictures showed Fosbury clearing the bar, set at six feet six inches, "by at least half a foot." Clearly the flop was anything but a flop. Why had the coach not recognized the superiority of the flop to the straddle earlier? Maybe the coach didn't see it because his own constraints told him it couldn't be true. But to his credit the coach finally got the picture. So the "Flop Club" doubled in membership—a jumper and his coach.

Then came the worldwide debut for the flop. On October 20, 1968, with more than eighty thousand spectators hushed in expectation and a worldwide television audience holding its breath, Fosbury rocked back and forth several times before sprinting toward the bar. By the time they exhaled, Dick Fosbury was not only an Olympic gold medalist, but he was also a U.S. and Olympic record holder. The Fosbury Flop became part of the sports lexicon.

Surely the high-jump Turtles would finally admit he was right and embrace flopping as the preferred technique, right? Wrong.

Instead, the near-religious conviction that "real" high jumpers didn't flop remained deeply entrenched in most coaches and athletes. When Fosbury began to fade (he never bested his Olympic heights and did not even make the 1972 U.S. Olympic team), the flop did, too. Coaches and parents called for the banning of the flop as too dangerous, ignoring the fact that pole-vaulters were landing on their necks and shoulders from much greater heights.

"The coaches and elite jumpers just had too many years of training already invested in straddling," Fosbury speculated later. "They just couldn't change." But thousands of junior-high and elementary kids saw Fosbury's winning moment on television "who didn't have any coaches to tell them not to do it like I did."

By 1976 all three medalists in the Olympic high jump were floppers. In 1980 thirteen of the sixteen finalists in the event flopped. So why weren't the other three finalists taking advantage of the break-through? Constraints—such as being overly resistant to change—die more slowly in some of us than in others.

Resisting change is common to many of us. Turtles don't like to rethink and overhaul routines that are comfortable and familiar. Fosbury's story is a vivid example of how opening our minds to new behaviors and opportunities can lead to greener pastures—or perhaps greater heights. If we keep doing what we're doing, we'll keep getting what we're getting. Are you willing to invest the energy and courage to look at your inner landscape and identify what is keeping you from achieving your equivalent of "clearing seven feet"?

Change: The Midnight Visitor

Lee Bason is one of my two partners at The Flippen Group, and he is about as resistant to change as a person can get. He is also as good a friend as I could ever have, and we have built a lot together.

But Lee has always hated change.

Several years ago I thought I might have a little fun with this particular personal constraint. You have to get a picture of what Lee's office looks like. He puts everything in the exact same place each night before he leaves. His office is always spotless and in perfect order.

One night after everyone had left the building, I went into his office. I picked up his pen and turned it around so that it was facing the opposite direction than it had been. That was it. That was all I touched.

The next day Lee came into my office the minute after he had walked into his own and asked, "Did someone use my office last night?"

"No, I don't think so. I was the last one to leave. Is there a problem?" I casually asked.

"No, I was just wondering." He hesitated, then turned and walked away.

That night I moved his stapler a few inches to the left, and the next day he was back.

"Flip, someone is using my office at night."

"Lee, why would someone come up here and break into the office so that they could sit at your desk? You need to lighten up!" was my response.

I continued to do the same thing for the next several days, and then I made the big jump. Lee had obviously been frustrated because he couldn't figure out what was going on. That night I picked up his phone and turned it around and hung it up facing the "wrong" way. That did it. He went over the top, and when he came in to tell me what had happened, I couldn't hold it in any longer. Everyone in the office had a good laugh because he can be so obsessive about things.

If we had to change his schedule, it frustrated him. If the airline was off schedule, it wrecked his day. If someone wasn't exactly on time, he was bothered. Everything had to be just right, and if it wasn't, he didn't handle it very well.

Change of any kind was a problem for Lee. But that's life, isn't it? Things change. Business changes, schedules change, goals change, the world changes. And we have to be able to adapt to it. Turtles, however, prefer to withdraw from the thought of change.

What if you lived during the time of horse-drawn buggies? Can you imagine being the greatest buggy whip maker in the area? Well, where are they now? It didn't matter how superior their deluxe model buggy whip was, a day came when the world changed, and there was no more need for buggies or buggy whips. If you can't change—you won't survive in today's world. It's that simple.

Lee knew this as well as anyone. We taught about change, and we led companies and schools through change. So he began to realize how embracing change would help him in his own life as well as allow him to be a better model for others. That meant addressing specific things that he did, such as resisting suggestions or requests for change in programs, schedules, habits, and processes.

Over the next year Lee grew tremendously. And over the past fifteen years, he has grown as much as anyone I have ever known. That is one of the main reasons he is a valued partner today.

People resist change for lots of reasons, including fear of the unknown, fear of failure, vested interests in things staying like they are, and anxiety tied to learning curves and trials with new things.

I have a business-operating philosophy that I live by on a personal level. "Whatever your operating paradigm is today, *it won't work for you in the future.*" We may not like it, but that doesn't change the reality. Change is an absolute given. Life moves on, and if you don't move with it, you will find yourself passed by and passed over in favor of others who can adapt to the changing needs of our culture.

I especially like what hockey great Wayne Gretzky said several years ago. A reporter asked him how he had broken every major hockey record. His response was simply, "I just skate where the puck is going to be."

There it is.

You head where things are going before they get there so you are ready and waiting by the time they arrive. No one ever won a hockey game by rushing to the spot where a fast-moving puck last *was.* The only things that I keep as a constant in my life are my morals, my principles, and my relationships. Everything else is subject to change.

So why do I call people who struggle with change *Turtles?*

Turtles try to cross the road, but they get scared. Something moves by them too fast, and they pull their head in to wait it out. Well, you know the end of that story. The lesson is: *if you want to make it to the other side of the road—stick your neck out and follow it.*

Are You a Turtle?

Check any of the following symptoms that occur and add up the total.

- [ ] Change and uncertainty make me nervous.
- [ ] I can think of instances in which I was resistant to something that I later found to be a better alternative.
- [ ] Tried and true is the safest path. Why take unnecessary risk?

☐ Things have a place they should go, and I don't like it when people are careless.

☐ Once I find something that works well for me, I tend to stick with it.

☐ If I need to switch directions, I need time to get comfortable.

☐ When people share new ideas with me, my first impression is to think of the reasons why the ideas won't work.

☐ I have been perceived as stubborn at times because I was reluctant to just dive in with the new direction others were proposing.

☐ I really like a stable routine.

☐ I like to plan out my days, projects, and even vacations, and I don't like people changing things later.

Turtle Tendencies?

Mark your total below.

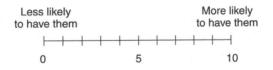

I am a Turtle—Help Me!

So I'm a Turtle—Help Me!

As an illustration to tie all of this together, I'll present an actual experiment that was undertaken. Place four monkeys in a room. Then put a ladder in the middle with some bananas at the top of the ladder. When one of the monkeys eventually begins to climb the ladder, shower all of the monkeys with water.

The next time one of the monkeys attempts to ascend the ladder, the other monkeys will stop him, and eventually no monkeys will even try to get a banana. Then remove one of the original monkeys and put a new monkey in the room. At some point it will attempt to get a banana, and the other monkeys will pull him back down.

Now replace another monkey. The recent addition will eventually wander toward the banana, and the other monkeys will stop him, and even the monkey who has never been sprayed will fully participate in the restraint!

What's especially interesting is that even after you replace the last monkey, and none has *ever* been sprayed, none of them will approach the ladder simply because that's the way they were taught. How unfortunate for them to be prisoners of their perceptions.

I'm not calling you a monkey, but I think the lesson is clear. Your bananas are waiting, so let's go get them!

Specific TrAction Steps

Here are some sample action steps you can take to start getting traction—today! Once you read all of the constraint chapters, if this is determined to be one of your killer constraints, then steps like these will be part of your TrAction Plan (to be built in chapter 15).

• I will start being even more open to new ideas. Even if I'm feeling some resistance, my first reaction will be positive and enthusiastic, such as "Wow, what I really like about where you are headed is that..." This will help demonstrate that I am really weighing the new direction. I will also make more statements such as, "I know I can be resistant to things at first, so I'm really not trying to do that in this case. My only real concern is that..." If I am still feeling resistance to being pushed in a new direction, maybe a question such as this would help: "Do you want me to think about it for a while or should we make a decision now?"

• I will start trying different things and say "let's try it" more often. I prefer more stable, tried-and-true choices, but there may be another option that I am missing out on. [State a specific habit or routine that you can focus on and then try something substantially different. Have someone who knows you well help come up with a fun idea of something new to try.]

• I will start further embracing different approaches along with people who think very differently. I usually don't enjoy sifting through a more unconventional idea, but there may be some part of the idea that is beneficial, so I need to better embrace "outside-the-box" ideas along with the people who usually have them.

How Can I Deal with a Turtle?

To effectively deal with someone like this, it is always important to make sure the person feels validated. Even the extreme of each constraint contains some positives, so make sure you communicate the positives also. Here are some potential strengths to validate: Enjoys continuity, Content with stability.

• Understand that Turtles have a need for stability, so if you want them to switch directions, preface the discussion with "We don't have to make a decision right now, but I wanted to plant a seed and have you think about it." Even just a few hours of being able to ponder an unexpected twist can allow them to be more receptive.

• If you are interacting with a Turtle who is expressing resistance to something new, continuing the discussion can sometimes make it worse, so be willing to walk away and revisit the discussion later. Turtles usually need more time to process their thoughts.

13 *Killer Constraint #9:*
Volcanoes (Aggressive, Angry)

Mike Tyson has probably undergone more psychological testing than any world-class athlete in the history of the world, which makes me curious: what were his interviewers expecting to discover?

The source of his aggression?

Why he told one interviewer that his basic impulse was to drive the bone of his opponent's nose deep into the back of his brain?

Why he declared, "I am an animal in the ring," after he chewed off a sizable chunk of Evander Holyfield's ear?

Aggression by itself isn't a constraint for a world-class boxer. It is Mike's combination of constraints, particularly his glaring lack of self-control, that makes him a danger to society and himself.

Mike Tyson's constraints began in his rootless upbringing and were reinforced during his formative years. In fact, a closer inspection of Mike's childhood gives us a greater understanding of his savage—and often bizarre—behavior.

By the time Mike reached nine years of age, he was an incorrigible kid with a shoplifting problem and little parental influence in his life. His father had disappeared early on, his mother died seven years later, and his male role models became a succession of drug dealers, thieves, and scam artists.

Eager for companionship, young Mike fell in with a street gang whose older members began calling the new recruit Fairy Boy because of his high-pitched, squeaky lisp. Mike fought back hard and gained a reputation in the 'hood as someone with a short fuse, earning respect and a pair of gold teeth when his two front incisors were knocked out. When the fifth grader wasn't defending himself, he was roughing up defenseless women. His favorite ruse was offering to help older women carry their groceries into apartment buildings, but once in the stairwell, Mike socked the terrified women in the jaw and escaped with their wallets.

At the age of twelve, Mike was handcuffed and shipped off to Tyron School for Boys, a juvenile detention center in upstate New York. Young Mike was built like a Staten Island tugboat—five feet eight inches tall and weighing 210 pounds. He tested out at a third-grade reading level in the sixth grade, however, and his sullen disposition and lack of verbal skills prompted others to think he was mentally retarded. Away from the only home he had ever known and cast into a prisonlike setting for hard-core juvenile delinquents, Mike closed ranks and defended his turf with the only weapons he could depend on—his fists.

Bobby Stewart, one of the social workers at Tyron, oversaw the center's boxing program. The former Golden Gloves champion recognized fists and fury when he saw them, and this young kid from Brooklyn's Brownsville neighborhood showed no fear each time he sparred in the ring or another school-yard fight. Stewart also recognized that young Tyson's odds of becoming a productive member of society were rather remote, given his background, aggression, and lack of education.

Stewart placed a phone call to Cus D'Amato, a legendary trainer who oversaw a stable of young fighters at his training facility in the Catskill Mountains, and described a special young boxer in his program who beat up all comers at Tyron. After witnessing only one sparring session, Cus anointed Mike Tyson the future heavyweight champion of the world. The kid was only thirteen.

New York State authorities didn't put up much of a fight when the respected trainer offered to take Tyson off their hands. Mike was given a room in Cus's house, and for the first time ever, he had someone who wanted to instill some direction into his life.

"I'm a creator," said D'Amato in an interview. "I discover and uncover, take the spark and fan it. When it starts to become a little flame, I feed it until it becomes a fire. When it becomes a fire, I feed the fire until it becomes a roaring blaze. When it becomes a roaring blaze, I put huge logs on it. Then you've really got a fire going."

Maybe a volcano would be a more fitting description.

Mike Tyson rose to the top of the professional boxing ranks, earning his first heavyweight championship belt at the age of twenty, when he knocked out Trevor Berbick. But research shows that "Iron Mike" was still a young child emotionally in those early years. He is said to have broken down in tears before major bouts and fought his nerves prior to the fight longer than he fought his opponents, though nearly all of them landed on the canvas in a stupor in the first round. As Mike took the fight game by storm, he defended his heavyweight championship ten times, until he inexplicably lost his title to Buster Douglas, in 1991.

Fury Outside the Ring

Life quickly spiraled out of control after Iron Mike was knocked off his perch, and this is when I started to become interested in him and his story. I'm not a huge boxing fan, but when Tyson was arrested for allegedly raping Desiree Washington, Miss Black America, in 1991, I sat up and took notice. Having worked with lots of troubled boys for most of my life, I could understand why a kid who had never felt love has no idea how to express his emotions except through anger and force.

My interest was in the personal constraints impacting his life. Clearly a certain amount of aggression is absolutely essential for success in some sports, especially boxing. But anyone who starts a brawl at weigh-in on the morning of a big fight or slugs his opponent at a press conference has obviously taken it too far. We expect people to contain themselves, to follow established rules of public decorum, just as we expect boxers not to start boxing until they hear the bell ring.

There is one more factor that we don't want to dismiss because it shows up in many people's lives when they reach a certain level of financial success. Since the mid-1980s Mike had earned an incredible $112 million; the downside is that he had spent $115 million, according to court records. Look at the money he threw away on cars, which was his greatest series of impulse buys. An accounting of his estate showed that he had spent $4.4 million on automobiles and motorcycles over the course of a few years. A necessary expense, he insisted, because fancy cars made him appealing to fancy women.

These days Iron Mike needs money, which is why we can expect him to continue doing the only thing he really knows: slug others into submission in the "square circle." Of course in these days of reality shows and sports celebrity marriages, it's anybody's guess what the next fight may look like.

I can't help but think about how sad this all is. Here is a young man with an incredibly broken life who is gifted with tremendous athletic ability. Through no actions of his own, he was born into a significant amount of dysfunction, and apart from perhaps two relationships in his life, he is alone. To survive he has to be a fighter in both the literal and figurative sense of the word. Tragic is the only word I can think of.

Is it any wonder that he is angry? Is it a surprise to anyone that a child who had to deal with a life like his turned to violence? Sadly, this is not a unique case, and I've seen it happen over and over with other broken and lonely people with these constraints.

Volcanoes are just that—they are volatile. They explode without much notice. This past summer I stood at the base of Mt. Vesuvius outside of Rome. Vesuvius blew up in A.D. 79 and destroyed Pompeii and all of its inhabitants. But let me give you a hint. There were warnings. Just days before there had been earthquakes, and in A.D.

62, seventeen years earlier, there had been a series of major earth-quakes that had rocked the entire region and destroyed many of the buildings there. Then one day it all came apart.

In many cases people are much like that. There are rumblings. You see them throw fits and rage about things, all the while boiling underneath. Then suddenly there is an explosion, and people get hurt.

Secondhand Smoke

Katie was in her early forties when she married Antonio, who was seven years younger and storybook "tall, dark, and handsome." Having been single many years, Katie was excited at the prospect of having a partner and friend to navigate the unexpected twists and turns of life that were still ahead.

After a whirlwind romance Katie and Antonio married and settled into the business of merging hearts, dreams, and living-room furniture. Katie knew that she was not walking into an idyllic world—her husband had been married once before, and he had described his five-year marriage as a tumultuous series of breakups and breakdowns that ended with Antonio walking out several times, then finally one day for good. She had thought it through and decided that he was worth the gamble.

Katie had come from a home marked by abandonment and physical abuse and had spent years working through her trust issues with men. She never dreamed that as a forty-three-year-old woman she would find herself dealing with the same fears she had known as a ten-year-old. But she did.

The only difference was that this volcano went off when she least expected it. Her father gave plenty of warning with his angry slamming and bellowing as he stormed around the house during one of his fits. Sometimes there was even time to hide and wait it out.

But this volcano was different. After the first eruption hit not even a year into the marriage, Katie realized that Antonio's constraint, like secondhand smoke, was as deadly to those around him as it was to himself.

Building Up Steam

Antonio and Katie each traveled frequently for their jobs, and one trip had them meeting in the same city, so they arranged to travel home on the same flight. They did not have seats together, so Antonio decided to see if he could switch his wife's seat and have her sit next to him on the aisle at the bulkhead, where there was plenty of room to relax. Realizing that her ticket showed a middle seat somewhere back in the plane's "Siberia" section, Katie suggested that they instead give up Antonio's seat on the bulkhead so whoever was kind enough to trade would be able to trade "up" rather than "down."

Antonio didn't like the idea and insisted on keeping his seat. Meanwhile the plane was slowly filling up, and the passenger who rightfully "owned" the seat for that flight arrived. Antonio said to him, "You wouldn't mind trading seats so my wife can sit next to me, would you?" The man hesitated for a moment, then graciously said, "I guess that would be okay." He took Katie's ticket, scanned the seat rows, and realized—too late—the bad deal he had agreed to, but he just grimaced and headed for the back. Embarrassed, Katie pleaded with her husband to give the man his seat and go with her to the back.

Antonio began to get loud, declaring the man was perfectly happy with the trade. He jumped up and walked halfway back to where the man was, calling out, "My wife thinks you are unhappy with your seat. But you're fine, right?"

The man replied, "Well, actually, I would prefer my aisle seat, but it's okay."

Antonio turned back to Katie. "See? I told you it was okay!" He continued to go on loudly, and by this time, everyone around them was annoyed by the noise and commotion. Katie slid down in her seat, hoping they wouldn't be asked to leave before the plane even took off. Antonio finished his tirade and went into a sullen silence, which would last for the three-hour flight and then continue as they drove home.

At the house they revisited the incident, and after an hour of arguing, apologies were made, and Antonio hugged his wife, resting his head on her shoulder. She held him and stroked his hair as they sat quietly together for about a half hour, glad it was finally over.

Although he generally confines his violence to his marriage and home, Katie told me about a recent banquet held by Antonio's company which was the scene of one of his latest fits. He didn't notice the company president walking up behind him as he let loose with a string of obscenities at Katie over a minor incident. Although the president didn't say much, Antonio continues to dig a deeper hole for himself with each indiscretion. Unless he chooses to change his direction, it is only a matter of time until an eruption occurs that will bury his dreams and plans forever.

Although physical differences can cause volcanic tendencies to be more dangerous when found in men, this constraint is just as devastating to relationships—especially with husbands and children—when displayed by women. Even minor daily frustrations left to simmer without a healthy way to explore and resolve them can build and create a volatile and stressful atmosphere that isn't healthy for anyone.

Remember, it's not about gender. It's about the personal constraint. You might also note that there aren't many people who want to live around volcanoes.

Are You a Volcano?

Check any of the following symptoms that occur and add up the total.

- ☐ When I'm stressed and under pressure, my frustration is obvious.
- ☐ Force and power are effective ways to reach people.

☐ I have a strong will to win, and I don't ever play to lose.

☐ I can get quite angry if pushed too far.

☐ It's hard for me to say "I'm sorry," and I definitely don't like being forced to say something.

☐ I speak my mind openly and directly. How other people feel about it is their business.

☐ If someone pushes on me, of course I'm going to push back.

☐ When I'm in a competitive situation, I get very serious.

☐ If you aren't pulling your weight, then you should get off the team.

☐ There are certain things you just don't want to say to me.

Volcano Tendencies?

Mark your total below.

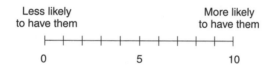

So I'm a Volcano—Help Me!

What's so bad about being competitive at times? Or even angry every once in a while? Nothing, as long as you are choosing to be competitive or angry. If you get in a disagreement and the next thing you know your heart is racing and voices are raised, then you probably aren't choosing to be a competitive participant in the discussion.

I'm actually competitive myself, and I've been that way for as long as I can remember. So, you might ask, if I'm still competitive, what am I doing writing this prescription? That depends on the goal. If my goal was to stop being competitive, then I certainly haven't accomplished that. My goal was simply to look for more win-win alternatives.

An old parable illustrates this perfectly.

A wise, gray-haired Cherokee sits down to reflect on life, and his grandchild walks up and sits down. The child is upset about losing a game, and with a slight smile, the grandfather says: "We all have a fight going on inside us. It is a raging fight between two wolves. One wolf represents anger, resentment, superiority, selfishness, and a hunger to win at all costs. The other wolf stands for compassion, humility, respect, generosity, and empathy."

The child thought about this for a while, and then asked, "Grandfather, which wolf will win?"

The grandfather pauses, takes a deep breath in and then out before answering, "Whichever one you feed."

Let me remind you (and myself) that it's okay to want to win, but let's make sure we are feeding both wolves. Otherwise you'll win, but there won't be anybody left to play with.

Specific TrAction Steps

• I will stop using these win-lose phrases in discussions: "Again..." "But..." "Like I said earlier..." and "No, what you said was..." Instead, I will substitute win-win responses such as "I see your point, so where do we go from here?" and "My memory is fuzzy, too, so I'm just making sure I understand everyone's perspective today."

• I will stop letting discussions escalate and become tense, committing to the fact that if I'm defensive then it is my fault, not someone else's. If the only way I can make my point is to talk louder, then I'm obviously not communicating well. Whenever I disagree with someone, I will pause for at least a few seconds before responding.

• I will stop trying to get the last word in a disagreement by being willing to be the person who simply says, "I think you're right" or "I was definitely wrong to..." or "I'm really sorry." For me to win means someone else has to lose, which isn't the best way to conclude a discussion.

• When I drive my car I will stop getting frustrated with other drivers, which stresses out those in the car with me. For one day I will drive five miles per hour below the speed limit, and as other people pass me, I will wave nicely while thinking about how I would normally be perceived by passengers and by other drivers.

How Can I Deal with a Volcano?

To effectively deal with someone like this, it is always important to make sure the person feels validated. Even the extreme of each constraint contains some positives, so make sure you communicate the positives also. Here are some potential strengths to validate: Competitive, Aggressive.

• When interacting with a Volcano, be especially careful of using any "trigger words" that can fluster him or her. Watch for shifts in body language or tone and apologize for any words that might not have come across well.

• If you sense a Volcano becoming upset, look for ways to de-escalate the discussion. Make efforts to maintain your composure and to also help the Volcano stay calm. Avoid any statements that could make him or her feel "cornered" because those feelings may be strong and undercontrolled.

14 *Killer Constraint #10:* Quick Draw (Low Self-Control, Impulsive)

Although Arnie has the discipline to work for hours on a project, he gets bored if a deal takes too long to put together. When he gets bored, he begins searching for the next deal, because in Arnie's mind, the *next* business opportunity will surely be his best. But that never seems to happen. Over the years he's pocketed a few bucks along the way, but when I caught up with him, he told me that he was working on his "best idea" ever—a shoo-in for his investors. But looking at his track record, that would be very unlikely.

Arnie has built buildings, developed real estate, sold rights for bottled water, worked in multilevel sales, and owned a management company, but he has never stuck with any venture long enough to make it truly successful. Without significant changes in his behavior, Arnie will always be chasing rainbows. The critical constraints for him are his low self-control and high need for change. Either way he is a moving target with someone else's money. And he is constantly moving.

So what can he do to fix this personal constraint in his life? First, Arnie must identify the constraint himself, which is what we call self-assessment (remember, this is difficult to do by yourself). Arnie has been blind to this for years. When I helped him walk through this process, he began to see the effect his constraints were having on his success. "Your constraint is your impulsive way of making decisions," I explained. "You don't stick with anything for very long." Although he had been told this in the past, it took hard data to make him really see it. He knew that he had been successful at many things, but he got bored easily and always moved on to something else. Now he had to agree to deal with the root: to get a grip on his constantly changing behavior. Then came the question I always hope to hear.

"So, what do I have to do?" he asked me.

Committing to the Process

I suggested making an accountability plan, where he would be responsible to someone who could hold his feet to the fire if he tried to make a move to greener pastures. "Perhaps your banker could get involved," I said. Arnie reluctantly took my advice. After much discussion, including some time with his wife (who reminded him that she knew this had always been a problem for him), Arnie agreed to the "conditions." He and his banker agreed that Arnie would stay with a particular project for the duration and that he would not move on to the next thing for at least six months *after* the end of the next project. As you can imagine this drove Arnie nuts. He was a true "Quick Draw" and didn't like being held accountable by his banker or his wife.

Now we theoretically had control over the issue of being too impulsive—the ability to stick with something for the duration. We had a grip on the problem and some accountability. Next came the step of moving forward, or what I call self-directing. Arnie threw himself into his next project and did well, although there were times he wanted to walk away as the project was nearing completion. But he hung in there. In fact, when the temptation became the greatest, he would call me, and we would talk about where he wanted to go with his life; this helped bring things back into focus.

This is a key to being successful with this constraint—keeping the goal in mind and staying focused on where you are going over time. Arnie was constantly changing and playing with new ideas. After we got this squared away, he has been extremely successful and is having more fun than ever.

Arnie confided recently that he misses the excitement of changing businesses every few years but that it has been worth it, as he is successful and providing for his family without the stresses and pressures that he was having before. His wife certainly enjoys the greater sense of stability, which helps them get along better.

It makes me wonder how many people have hit on a great idea and then blown it, for no other reason but that they didn't stick with it. Their personal constraint of low self-control got in their way and hindered their ability to deliver something that might have changed their life as well as the lives of others.

Quick Draw Comes in All Sizes

Most of us don't get "do overs" in life. I love the movie *Groundhog Day,* starring Bill Murray. Every morning—until he gets it right—is a "do over" for Bill. If only I had some days like that. I remember a day when I was a kid playing in Little League, and I had the chance to pitch in a big game. But I was grounded. Life is not fair. There is a tooth fairy, but where is the baseball fairy? You know, the fairy who comes in and makes everything right just when the bad guys (parents) are messing with your most important moment. I was grounded. How could this have happened? I was twelve years old, and life was baseball. But what did being grounded have to do with life or my future? Simply this: I had a constraint. I didn't know it was a constraint at the time, but I knew I had a problem, which was that I didn't like to do my homework. I didn't study because baseball was too important and "demanded" too much of my attention. The truth is that lots of things caught my attention, but homework wasn't one of them, since learning didn't come easily to me. So I put off homework and did the things that were more important to me (and that I was more success-ful at)—like baseball.

But really homework was just a symptom. The real problem was my distractible nature and lack of self-discipline. I did not have the ability to say to myself, "Do your homework." Punishment didn't have much effect, nor did failing.

Of course I did go on to college, and I completed my degrees to practice as a psychotherapist, and I now own and run a successful company, but not doing my homework did have a profound impact on me. It kept me from making good grades, which in turn kept me from playing on the baseball team in high school and later in college. I couldn't get into a school that had a baseball team and didn't get to play then, either. My poor study habits affected my grades in col-lege as well, and had it not been for some great professors, I would not have gone on to graduate school. Although I have experienced a good measure of success, I know that my life would certainly be farther along had I understood early on the far-reaching effects of my constraints.

It wasn't until I was in my twenties that I got serious about deal-ing with my lack of self-control. I worked hard at the things I wanted to work at but procrastinated on the things I didn't. I still need to focus on exercising self-control and probably will until my last day. At times I am too impulsive, and I can be too quick to change some-thing that is really working well, simply because I don't take the time to think through the impact my actions will have on the rest of our company. Low self-control can also have a tremendous impact on your decision making and approach to finances.

Quick Draw and Money

It was late in the day, and I had seen a full schedule of patients, in-cluding early morning stops at Greenleaf Psychiatric Hospital. My final patient was new, and I had little idea as to what the presenting problem would be. Angie Roberts was in her early twenties, attractive, and smartly dressed. You couldn't help but notice her elegant sense of fashion and style. She could not have been better put together as she came through the door.

We began our session like most others, reviewing her forms and discussing family information and her new job. Angie was single, and that was one of the points that she said she wanted to discuss. After going through the rest of the forms, I asked what she wanted to focus on first. "Why have you come to see me and how can I help you?"

Angie leaned forward and began to tell me about her boyfriend and their relationship. They had been together for more than two years, and she was getting concerned about where it was going. He wasn't appearing as interested as she had hoped he would be, and she didn't know how to move things along. It wasn't a matter of their relationship having problems as much as it was about his not asking the right questions, like "Will you marry me?"

Angie had no idea what she could do that might help her deal with the stress she was feeling. They got along fine and had a good time together. They had been to each other's homes many times and had met each other's parents. Everything seemed perfect—so what was the problem? Why wasn't he asking her "the question"?

In fact, he had seemed to avoid it more the longer they went together. Obviously this was beginning to weigh on her, and she had to either learn how to deal with it or find a way to get her boyfriend to bring the subject up. The last thing she wanted to do was ask for a proposal.

That became our goal for therapy. *How do I deal with a long-term relationship that is satisfying but doesn't seem to be going anywhere?* I was wondering, too. Why wasn't her boyfriend popping the question? What was there in the relationship or perhaps in his mind that was holding him back? I had seen more than enough young men who really struggled with making long-term commitments. They usually had their reasons, and even if I didn't agree with them, they were still reason enough to not ask for marriage. So what was the deal this time?

During our next session we discussed any issues that Angie might know about, and she truthfully couldn't come up with a reason that he wouldn't ask her to marry him. It was frustrating for her to say the least. Here she was—stuck with no proposal in sight. She was going to lots of weddings that year; they just weren't hers.

During our session I asked her, "What would he say if I asked him why he isn't proposing?" Her first response was, "I have no idea—maybe you should do that!" But then she thought about it a moment and added, "Well, he might say it's because he doesn't have enough money or he's waiting till he's more secure financially. He seems to worry about money a lot."

I asked what he did for a living, and she indicated that he had a good job with a land-development company. He had finished his MBA and had been working for a couple of years. Angie said he didn't have any debt with school because his parents made good money, and they had put him through school, including his graduate work. Besides that he had a car he had paid cash for, and he didn't seem to live beyond his ability to pay his bills. Overall, it sounded like he was fairly responsible with money, so that didn't seem to be the problem. Hmmmm... *Unless...*

"Angie, how are you with finances? Do you have any debt, or do you pay for things as you go?" I asked.

Looking away she said she had some debts but that she could manage and they weren't a problem. But her response needed more attention, so I pressed on. "Do you have any debt?" After a minute she looked at me and said that she thought she had around seven thousand dollars of credit-card debt. "On which card?" I asked. "Well, I have about seven thousand on my MasterCard and maybe that much on my Visa card," she quietly added.

Okay. *Now,* we were getting somewhere. "Do you have any other credit cards or bills that you get statements on?" "I get bills from some department stores that aren't on my credit cards, but I always pay them when I get them," she replied. "Do you pay them off or do you pay the minimum each month?" I asked. "I try to pay something on each one of them each month, but some months I can't because I have to pay on the others or they will turn it over to collections," she said.

"Angie, have you ever lied about your finances when someone asked you about what you owed or how you were with your money?" I asked. "No," she assured me. Then I asked, "Have you told me everything that you owe or have you left some things off the list?" At that point she started crying and said that she hadn't told me everything. In fact, "I guess I just lied about telling you everything, didn't I?"

"Um, yep. Now tell me why you would lie to me about your finances when you know that I am not going to judge you or do anything that would hurt you in any way. Why would you not share something when you are seeing me so that I can help you with whatever we need to deal with?" I asked. As she began to cry softly, she said through the tears, "I didn't want you to think badly of me, so I didn't want to tell you that I'm not good with money and I have a lot of debt from credit cards." When the whole story finally came out, Angie had over sixty thousand dollars' worth of credit-card debt, and she was only twenty-five years old.

As we took apart her spending habits, I quickly learned that she made most of her purchases on impulse and over 95 percent of them seemed to be on depreciating items like clothes and meals and personal-care products. I teased her that she might consider going into merchandising because all the products she had tried over the years would have made her an expert by now. We laughed but knew that it was painfully true.

The next item on the agenda was to find out what her boyfriend had to say about her spending. We invited him to our next session, and I asked him what he thought was the number-one thing that she could do to grow as a person. His response was very insightful.

"Well, what I think is holding her back is her inability to say no to herself when she wants something." This was a young man who knew what was going on, and he knew what it was doing to her. He went on to say, "She is hurting herself and us when she doesn't deal with this. She has way too much debt, and it scares me. What if we were married and she did this? I couldn't live with collections calls or not being able to pay the bills. That would drive me nuts."

There it was, plain as day. He couldn't have been any clearer about why he hadn't proposed. And he was right. I would have had a hard time asking someone to marry me if I knew that she was bringing sixty thousand dollars' worth of debt into the marriage as well as the behaviors that had gotten her into that mess. This was another case of "Quick Draw," but this time it would have been appropriate to have written "Quick Withdraw."

Angie was paying over 16 percent on all of her credit-card debt, and she was struggling to make the minimum payments at that rate. It would take her another fifteen years to pay off her debts if she kept it up at that pace. Of course she had an alternative. She could declare bankruptcy and move on.

In the last five years, we have seen a steady rise in the number of bankruptcies in this country. And why is that? It's because we make credit easily available, and we don't do much to teach people self-control. "You can have it now!" is the slogan of this age. In fact, you really don't even have to pay for it—at least not until January 1 or whatever magic date they pick.

I asked Angie to make an appointment with her banker. She said she would and then she asked me what she was going to talk to him about. "Well," I said, "I want you to ask him for a loan so you can buy some pizza for your party this weekend."

"What?" she exclaimed. "You want me to get a loan for a pizza? I don't understand." Then I explained to her that was what she had been doing. Every time she paid for a meal with her credit card, she was financing that meal, so why not go ahead and ask her banker for a loan? She had been paying 16 percent to finance her pizzas, and she could get a better deal with her banker if she would just ask for it.

Crazy, isn't it?

But that is what people are doing, and it doesn't seem to matter how much money they have, they still get themselves into more debt.

I have other young friends who are in the same boat—not that age has anything to do with it. They are putting off marriage because they don't want the risk that comes with marrying into high debt. Why get married and be responsible for the debt when you can just live together and skip the hassle? I suspect that would leave some people feeling that they are an unwanted burden except for the immediate rewards they can bring to the relationship.

Quick Draw comes in all forms. It could be impulsive decisions about money or career decisions or relationships—but it all boils down to the same thing. Do you make good decisions or are you too quick to make any decision? Let me go over that again. It may also be that you are "too quick" to make *any* decision and perhaps you should consider not making decisions until you have a better grip on yourself. If you don't "get a grip," you might end up paying a lot more than 16 percent for it. You could be selling your own happiness in the future so that you can finance a pizza today.

Are You a Quick Draw?

Check any of the following symptoms that occur and add up the total.

- ☐ I love trying new things.
- ☐ I need creative outlets to feel fulfilled.
- ☐ I have a tendency to leave projects or relationships that get difficult.
- ☐ I struggle with finances—impulse buys, shopping addictions, or lack of planning.
- ☐ Working in a stable, mundane environment can be emotionally draining.
- ☐ It is hard for me to stay on task once I lose interest.
- ☐ I am spontaneous and get bored with repetition very easily.
- ☐ My impulsive nature is a source of conflict in my relationships.
- ☐ I'm good at starting things but never seem to finish a lot of them.

☐ I might not think through an idea fully, but the details can be figured out later.

Quick-Draw Tendencies?

Mark your total below.

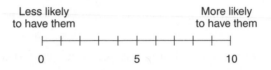

So I'm a Quick Draw—Help Me!

From my perspective three words come to mind that accurately describe my episodes of creativity: fresh, fun, and frenzied!

Some of my coworkers who value stability more than I do actually use three different words: uncontrollable, whirlwind, and destructive. Can you believe they would say that to me? One coworker recently coined a term for my episodes: "creativity seizures"! I definitely feel a creativity hangover after juggling too many ideas and seeing all of them hit the ground.

Your catalyst may not be creativity, but the net effect is that all of us who struggle in this area move too quickly at times. Maybe you start a lot of things and finish only a few or maybe you make impulsive decisions or speak without thinking through the impact on others.

When it comes to making impulsive decisions, if you find that others are resisting your ideas, here are the three most common explanations for this: (1) you haven't communicated the idea well, (2) the timing isn't right, or (3) you're wrong. Another thought is that you may have established a track record of frequently failed efforts that cause others to think twice about your latest brainchild, no matter how good it is. The bad news is all of these have to do with you! But I'm not here to applaud the idea killers out there, I just want us to look at our role in this ongoing tension.

A simple step is to not talk to anyone about an idea until you have written it down in a journal and waited one week. Then after a week you'll probably be better able to determine the idea's potential—that is, assuming you can find the journal! Also be careful of interrupting people, because sometimes your mouth may be two steps ahead of you. Regardless, be willing to embrace people who will give you honest feedback.

Specific TrAction Steps

Here are some sample action steps you can take to start getting traction—today! Once you read all of the constraint chapters, if this is determined to be one of your killer constraints, then steps like these will be part of your TrAction Plan (to be built in chapter 15).

• I will stop interrupting people. For one day I will not say anything in a conversation or in a meeting until there have been two seconds of silence. This will allow me to step back and see who was able to speak up and also notice that maybe some of the points I would have made weren't necessary. I will ask someone once a week, "How well have I been listening lately?" and have the person grade me on a one-to-ten scale.

• I will finish what I start. I get more energy from new ideas than from ideas that have been in place, but quite often my new ideas end up being at the expense of something valuable and effective. I will make more statements such as "If the timing isn't right on this, I am more than happy to table it for now." And I will ask the people I interact with the most this question once a week: "Have I been changing directions too quickly?"

• I will stop acting on impulse. If I have a new idea, I will write it in a document and then, after a week, review the idea again and decide if it is still worth pursuing. In addition I will stop involving other people too quickly in ideas or projects so that I don't take them off task. Instead of being defensive about them, I will embrace tough questions and before moving forward intentionally solicit feedback from the people who ask them.

How Can I Deal with a Quick Draw?

To effectively deal with someone like this, it is always important to make sure the person feels validated. Even the extreme of each constraint contains some positives, so make sure you communicate the positives also. Here are some potential strengths to validate: Adaptable, Can act quickly.

• If a Quick Draw person is sharing an idea, be sure to validate it with a response such as "I need to write this down, and we can make time to review it in more detail later. Are we needing to make a decision right now?" Maybe even saying, "Let's hold that thought for a few days" could help them feel heard and not cause you to feel immediate pressure. Be especially careful of being perceived by Quick Draws as being overly resistant to change. If you work with a Quick Draw frequently, ask questions such as "Do you feel like we are moving forward quickly enough?"

• If a Quick Draw person makes an impulsive decision, take into account timing in confronting them. Even if a decision is wrong, it may be wise to try to make the best of it, as opposed to being perceived as a critic. Because they want to be successful despite at times reacting too quickly, they will be open to information and details that will help them make a better decision. It's just important that this information is shared effectively so it doesn't sound judgmental. Quick Draws don't want to be wrong; they are simply reacting to something they really think needs to be different. Be sure that you validate the positives of this trait just as they should validate the positives of yours.

PART
III

Overcoming Personal Constraints

15 Building Your TrAction Plan

Everything we have been examining so far has brought us to...
TrAction. This is how we spell *traction*—to emphasize the
action.

If we don't act—then we don't become.

It is the "becoming" that is most important. In that respect I hope
that your reasons and the desire you have for personal growth compel
you to TrAction.

Why is this piece so critical? Primarily because we are all so
busy that if we don't make the leap from concept to plan, we will
quickly forget the information, no matter how life changing it may
be. Have you ever noticed your best intentions were not enough to get
something done, simply because you were too busy reacting to life
and putting out fires that were not on your agenda? Having a written
TrAction Plan is the best way to live by design rather than by default
and to provide a systematic and steady path for growth.

We coined the term TrAction because we want you to do more
than add activities to your task list. We want you to achieve TrAction,
that force that will give teeth to your efforts and continue moving you
forward on a specific course of action.

The Purpose of a Plan

The previous chapters all laid the foundation for this critical piece of your growth process—a one-page TrAction Plan. (As mentioned earlier in the book, you can download a blank TrAction Plan from www.flipsidebook.com.) This document will include:

1. Your ultimate goal for this process
2. A list of your strengths
3. Your top one or two personal constraints
4. Specific TrAction steps
5. An accountability plan

I want you to know that I have had to learn how to work with this process, as it goes against my nature somewhat. I tend to move through things too quickly at times, but doing the work step-by-step has held great rewards for me personally. Take your time and do it right. Don't rush through this process or you will end up dealing with a few surface issues without really making the deeper changes that last.

Understanding the goal—or your desired end result—is the most powerful part of the process of change. After many years of working with patients and clients in the area of personal constraints, I was excited to discover a management expert named Eliyahu Goldratt who was doing similar work in the corporate world. His book *The Goal* tells the fictional story of a factory where resources repeatedly pile up at bottlenecks in the production process. He showed that these bottlenecks, or constraints, impose their limitations on the overall system and determine its pace.

Reading through Dr. Goldratt's discussion of how systems work and why they develop bottlenecks (places where work piles up or slows down) was further confirmation of my studies about the same processes in people. Why do talents back up and not come out? Why can't people operate at a higher level in their lives? What are the real bottlenecks behind failed plans?

Dr. Goldratt goes on to present a "thinking process" for each of the following questions that apply just as readily to individual change as they do to a production system:

1. What to change?
2. What to change to?
3. How to cause the change?

Step 1: Establish the Goal

The answer to the first question is easy: we want to change the personal constraints that are most impacting our performance. The second question requires a little more thought: What do you want to change *to?* Or what is your *"behavioral goal"*?

Using one or two sentences, summarize the key aspects of your desired end result. Write it from the heart and make it yours.

Being a Great Dad

The first night home following the birth of my son Matthew set the tone—in many ways—for the rest of my life. I examined who I was at that time and where I wanted to go. I knew I wanted to be a good father to him, and I had a pretty good idea of what things needed to change for that to happen. I made sure to write it all down.

That was my first goal—to be a great dad. I have other goals as well: to be a great husband to Susan, to be a great boss to my staff, to be a successful educator. You'll find that as you work on your personal constraints, each of them impacts different areas of your life in similar ways. For example, let's say that to become a great dad and husband I want to become a more caring and less dominant person. I would say that: *"I am going to let those close to me know that I value them and their opinions and that their thoughts and needs are more important to me than are my own. I am going to learn to put others first and to consider them and their needs in my decisions."*

Other Sample Behavioral Goals

1. I commit to a clear focus on those things in my life that I value most: my family, health, happiness, and career.
2. In order for me to balance my life, I will make whatever changes are necessary to be my best, so that others can be their best.
3. Through measurable, meaningful behavior, I will begin to show my family, friends, and coworkers that I can be counted on.
4. I will become someone who follows through on commitments and who completes tasks that I start.
5. I want to increase my leadership performance, efficiency, and fulfillment by breaking self-critical behaviors. I will learn from my mistakes and then let them go.
6. I want to be thought of as someone who values other people and brings them together for a common good. To accomplish this I will modify the overbearing part of my personality to be more open and accepting of others.

Step 2: Identify Strengths

This section is a list of strengths you possess, those that you will build on. Your growth will be driven by these strengths. If someone is competitive, then yes, it's possible that he or she is too competitive at times, but in this section just list the word "competitive" and move on.

Since we established that it is impossible to self-assess without getting confirming feedback from others, it is recommended that you find someone you trust who could help you with the complete process, starting with your strengths. Ask your "Feedback Partner" to make a similar list so you can compare and take note of any discrepancies between your list and his or hers.

Don't restrict yourself to the list below. In fact, I'd prefer that you make your initial lists without reviewing the words below. But if you are like many people, after a while you can run out of ideas, so this list should be able to spur some thoughts:

Nurturing

Competitive

Leadership Ability

Creative

Conversational

Sees Positives

Approachable

Careful

Unselfish

Independent

Good Self-Control

People Focused

Detail Oriented

Dependable

Patient

Thoughtful

Empathetic

Decisive

Logical

Enjoys People

Sensitive

Confident

Good First Impression

Humorous

Can Defer When
    Necessary

Follow Through

Open to New Ideas

Team Oriented

High Expectations

Relaxed

Responsible

Good at Improving
    Things

Outgoing

Thorough

Thinks Outside
    the Box

Innovative

Supportive

Visionary

Driven

Social Presence

Energetic

Enjoys Change
    and Variety

Enthusiastic

Flexible

Organized

Humble

Optimistic

Spontaneous

Shares Spotlight

Analytical

Efficient

Perceptive

Resilient

Calm

Stable

Influential

Rule Respecting

Step 3: Target Top Two Constraints

In this step go back through the checklists that you completed with each chapter of the Top 10 Killer Constraints. I want you to identify the top two killer constraints that showed up the strongest out of all your checklists (if you have only one, then just work with that one). Remember, even if you checked only a few symptoms here and there, look for the areas you see as your weakest areas to start. And as I mentioned earlier, it's not just the total on each assessment that determines the magnitude of the constraint, so even if you checked only a few it could still be a significant constraint for you.

Write down your top two killer constraints.

1. _____

2. _____

This section is a summary of the one or two constraints you are going to work on. If there were three, leave the third for later. Even if the scoring was close, choose the two you believe are the most impacting and start there. You do not need to overwhelm yourself with change at this point.

Be Brutally Honest

Write down a couple of sentences that will allow you to specifically think about how these two constraints are impacting your life. See if you can think of a specific situation where these two constraints have actively (and negatively) affected your life. If you are like me, when I started thinking about it, I could think of several situations where my constraints had caused hurt to those around me, and I needed to change.

Step 4: Specific TrAction Steps

The fourth step is fairly simple, but it requires commitment.

Now you're beginning to develop a plan for yourself. A plan is the difference between wandering around without directions and using a map to see where the destination is—and the shortest route to get there.

This section will be composed of simple action steps that will help you break the toughest personal constraints. First, each step needs to be behavioral and specific. Let me share with you some of the things I have done with my own personal constraints.

Like many entrepreneurs I have fairly high self-confidence. I also have a fairly high need for change, in addition to low self-control. The high self-confidence is a good thing for the most part, but having a high need for change combined with low self-control makes for some interesting times. I tend to think I am right and can be easily impatient with others. My pace is fast, and I like to be moving all the time. Being creative means that I come up with lots of ideas, and having high self-confidence means that I think my ideas are really "brilliant"—and although I would never really say that, it's what someone with my constraints would think! (By the way, even as I write this, I feel embarrassed that I have had these constraints. But to address them honestly frees me to take the action I need to get beyond them.)

How do my constraints play themselves out? Let's walk through a typical meeting at my company's office, say, a meeting with the "new product" team. We start our meeting as usual—on a positive note, where several people share good news on a project or even something personal such as a child winning an award or getting a good grade. This usually takes a few minutes. If it runs much longer than that, I can feel impatience start to kick in, and I begin to wonder, "When are we getting down to business?"

Next, someone presents the product ideas to be discussed and asks if there is anything new that we need to consider. Of course I have something new to discuss because I read something or heard something or dreamed something up during the night. "Have you written anything down on that idea that we could go over?" asks the discussion leader. "No," I have to answer, since my low self-control has caused me to get excited about the idea's concept without taking the time to prepare my case. I secretly wonder why they can't just hear the idea and respond to it during the meeting. It doesn't take long for me to begin to get frustrated with the slow pace of the meeting and the requests for more information. But, because I really love and respect my team members, I try to work through it all with as much patience as I can muster. I know that they are doing everything they can to tend to me and my latest "stroke of brilliance," but clearly my constraints are showing.

So what do I work on? First, I need a basic behavioral plan that will allow me to get some control over what is going on. I need to find practical ways to curb my tendencies toward impulsiveness, especially when it involves my ideas. So I make some decisions. I decide that I won't come to the meeting with a new idea unless I have written it down and submitted it to the discussion leader prior to the meeting. Then I make a rule for myself that, once I present the idea, I must let the group discuss it without trying to push or sell it to them. I'll respond to questions but will do my best not to pressure the others when it doesn't look like things are going "my way."

Next, I decide I need to better appreciate the tons of work done by my team that creates the backdrop for each new idea I come up with (and realize that they are still working through all the follow-up tasks of my last idea). I attempt to do this by asking questions about what they are currently working on and listening carefully as they share areas of challenge or difficulty. To continually keep their part of the workload in sight helps me remain realistic with timelines and expectations.

Last, I let the team decide the priorities that need to be worked on at this time. This part is especially difficult for me, because discipline is not acquired overnight. But if I really value my team and believe that I have the right people doing the right things, then why wouldn't I let them do what they do best—which is to execute great projects?

After listing these very specific behavioral steps, I then tell some of my team what I am working on and give them specific things that I am going to change so that I can become a better team member.

As the founder of the company, I have a lot of influence over what happens. I need to use that influence to grow my team so that we are each using our gifts in the best way. I am not an execution guy. I hate details, and I get bored quickly trying to think through all of the various parts of something. Why wouldn't I let those who are gifted at that part of the process tell me what will work and how long and how much money it will take?

Now, to be honest, that was not a hypothetical meeting I just described. It was an actual meeting, complete with the process that I am working through right now. I need to make these changes if my team is to perform better. I understand that I can be disruptive without wanting to be, and I can get people and resources off task without much difficulty. I also know that "no company can rise above the personal constraints of its leadership," and that would be me. If I want my company to be better, then *I* have to be better. It's simple but profound. There is no other way around the process. If a company or family or team or organization is to grow, then the leadership has to be committed to growing, too.

As you see, my steps included specific behaviors and specific times (prior to and during meetings). Only one element was missing: I needed an accountability partner, an outside observer who could help me measure my progress. I picked two partners and asked them to rate me on a one-to-ten scale after each meeting. I have made great progress as a result of this process. At least that's the feedback I'm getting—and my partners don't tend to cut me much slack, either.

While I am on the subject of TrAction Plans, let me quickly tell you how we use them in our company. Every person in our company is on a personal-growth plan at any given time. Each quarter we draw up our action steps to target the constraints we want to work on for that three-month period. The plan can cover any area—professional or personal—as long as you are focused on a personal constraint that you are looking to break in some area of your life. We each have a few specific actions that we are making to improve, and we each have an accountability partner with whom we check each week. At the end of each month, we rate each other on how well we are improving, complete with a scorecard on how we are doing. I get one just like everyone else, and I can tell you exactly how I am doing on my plan and whether I am tending to the things I have committed to change.

We aren't real big on end-of-the-year evaluations because I don't believe in waiting a year to give someone feedback. I want my feedback as soon as I can get it so I can change as soon as possible. Also, this process doesn't take much time. We move through it quickly because the goal is not to waste time rating and evaluating—the goal is results. And it works. We are continually growing, and others around us know what we are working on so that they can be supportive in the process.

The fact is that you can think your way to a new way of behaving or you can behave your way to a new way of thinking. Let me explain. If you work on your thinking, it will eventually influence your behavior, but this takes time. I prefer to change behavior first and have your thinking come along behind it. I have found it's easier to steer a moving car than one that is parked. Changing your behavior is faster, and it means more to others when they can see your behavior changing right in front of them.

Let me ask you a question: do you need psychotherapy?

Although being a "shrink" is part of what I do, I personally don't think most people really need to see a professional. In most cases a good spouse can give you all the insight you need for change, and a good friend can do wonders at holding you accountable for doing it.

Let's keep it real simple.

I CAN do things that I remember, and I CAN do things that make sense to me.

I CAN'T do lots of things at once. Working on a few things is much easier than trying to change my whole life in one week.

So remember to KISS it: Keep It Simple, Simple!

Some thoughts on building the plan:

1. Use specific behaviors:
   - **Don't** use general terms like "be nice."
   - **Do** use behaviors like saying, "Thank you for letting me know your thoughts on..."
2. Use specific times:
   - **Don't** say, "When I can."
   - **Do** say, "Each morning I will" or "Two times each day I will."
3. Use stop and start statements:
   - "I will **STOP** raising my voice when I am angry."
   - "I will **START** asking more questions about the other person's feelings and listen to the person when he or she is telling me what they feel."

Once you pick the one or two constraints you are going to work on, FIRST try to come up with some action steps on your own BEFORE using any of the sample TrAction steps at the end of each constraint chapter. Your final TrAction Plan really needs to be in your language and apply to your goals in life, so customize heavily.

As a rule of thumb, five or six total action steps is a good number to shoot for.

Step 5: Accountability

The last section is the written accountability plan. I can make all kinds of personal commitments, but without someone to help me by holding me to my plan, it's very unlikely I'll make a lasting change. Use this section to designate your partners in identifying your strengths and top two constraints and then whom you will send this plan to. Include how often you will ask for feedback and what the feedback will look like.

Keys to Success:

- Work with a trusted partner and be accountable.
- Have someone work through the strengths and constraints with you to make sure you're covering areas you can't see (remember the mirror illustration).
- Ask someone to check with you.
- Make your checkup a regular event (but keep it simple—during a busy week an e-mail is a great alternative).

When it comes to formatting the plan, I know some of you are very detailed and others wouldn't want a page full of itemized lists. We have tried many plan variations, and I have found that almost everyone benefits from the structure presented here. Here is a sample TrAction Plan:

TrAction Plan Sample
Terry

Goal:

To view myself in a completely new way, undoing negative thought patterns that have been reinforced over the years. I will stop beating myself up, because it not only hurts me, but it also impacts those around me.

Strengths:

Nurturing	*Unselfish*	*Team Player*	*Sensitive*
Humble	*Loyal*	*Patient*	*Orderly*
Relaxed	*Follow Through*		

Key Constraints: *Ostrich and Marshmallow*

Being low in self-confidence and overly nurturing play them-selves out in my relationships, in my emotional stability, and in my work performance. I want to begin chipping away at some of the destructive habits I have formed, rewiring my view of myself, which will help me avoid spiraling downward emotion-ally along with being perceived as hypersensitive to criticism.

TrAction Steps: *I will:*

<u>*Start*</u> *taking responsibility for the self-defeating language I use internally. Phrases like "I'm the worst at ..." and "That was so stupid of me" are no longer acceptable, and when I have those thoughts, I will substitute more positive language.*

<u>*Start*</u> *reading the ten strengths in my TrAction Plan every day, and one month from now I will be able to recite the list and truly embrace each strength.*

Stop saying "I'm sorry" when it is unnecessary. It creates an awkward situation, and it causes me to be perceived as needy.

Start being more expressive with people, especially those in my outer circle. When I walk into rooms, I will confidently approach people with a genuine smile, a firm handshake, solid eye contact, etc., striving to have a presence without feeling a need to be someone I am not.

Stop avoiding conflict, which causes me to not say what I really think, to bottle up issues until they get worse, and to not give feedback because I don't want to risk hurting people. This trait also makes it difficult to set appropriate boundaries on my helpfulness, so I will start being able to say no when appropriate.

Accountability Plan: _So that I can get TrAction, I will either call or e-mail Kate and Chris each week for the next twelve weeks, entrusting them with an honest update of my progress. At least once a month, I will ask them if they have suggestions on my growth process._

TrAction Plan For _____

Goal: _____
_____
_____

Strengths:
1)   6)
2)   7)
3)   8)
4)   9)
5)   10)

Two Constraints Summary:
1)
2)

TrAction Steps:
1)_____
_____
2)_____
_____
3)_____
_____
4)_____
_____
5)_____
_____
6)_____
_____

Accountability Plan:_____
_____
_____

16 Constraints Are Personal: My Story

Throughout this book I've asked you to do a lot of very personal soul-searching. And I've also revealed parts of my own story and my own constraints. But it's not fair to ask you to be totally up-front about your constraints without telling you a bit more about mine.

Personal constraints are extremely real to me because I have had to overcome so many of them on the way to becoming who I am today. Although some constraints arrived with me in this world—such as dysgraphia and dyscalcula, which limited me in the area of math—others came in through my parents and upbringing, and finally, many were consequences of my own choices and priorities along the way.

Like every set of parents who struggles with unresolved issues in their lives, my parents did their best. I share this story not to dishonor them in any way but to let you know where the deep convictions I hold regarding personal constraints began. I love my parents and family but also know that all of us have stuff that impacts others. My parents' issues impacted me and my siblings in many ways. With permission, I'd like to share some of those experiences.

My dad was married to another woman when he had an affair with my mother, and she became pregnant with me. My paternal grandmother (a genteel Southern ranch lady) threw a genuine Southern hissy fit when she found out an illegitimate grandson was on the way. She insisted that the right thing to do was for my dad to divorce his first wife and marry my mother, which he did.

Now this is not the best way to start a happy family. Worse yet, I was at the center of the whirlwind, having "caused" all the upheaval the new marriage brought with it.

Being a child, I didn't understand that the resulting anger and unhappiness in my home was not a normal part of growing up. I did the best I could to just stay out of my parents' way.

Discovering Purpose

In the second grade underlying issues began to surface. I discovered I couldn't learn to read. I quickly fell behind in my classes, lost interest in learning, and started getting into trouble both at school and at home.

At the end of the second-grade year, my teacher took me aside. She said the school principal wanted to meet with five boys to talk with them about a special opportunity. We met with the principal during class time, and she said, "Each year, we pick a few children to help the first graders get started in the second grade. If you boys feel like you can do this, you will need to get your parents' permission, and then we will see who gets chosen to help them before the next school year begins. But you must get permission to do this."

I was excited that I was one of just a few who might be chosen and raced home to see if my mom would allow me to do it. My parents both agreed, and I was chosen. That next year was a good year for me. I remained in my same second-grade classroom, and although I still struggled, especially with math, I was thriving under the extra attention and sense of purpose.

Years later, when I was attending college, my mother and I were talking about my days at Anderson Elementary School. She told me they had started me in school a year early, but it hadn't worked out because I was not at the same maturity level as the other kids in my class. She then told me that I had been held back in the second grade because I couldn't read.

I was dumbstruck. *"What?"*

"Don't you remember being held back in the second grade?" she asked.

My face registered shock and disbelief. *"I wasn't held back! I was picked to help first graders!"* I nearly shouted at her.

I have to confess that my mother really caused a jolting paradigm shift that day. All those years I had thought I had been given an important and prestigious assignment in grade school, when in fact, I had failed second grade.

Of course my mother did not realize the contrast between her brusque words and the positive presentation of the principal to an impressionable six-year-old. Her own lifelong fears and struggles had kept her from being close to me, and I had never received much affirmation or encouragement from her as a child. I was fortunate that my second-grade teacher, Mrs. Ruthie Matthews, stepped into that role. She taught me how to read, encouraged me, and helped me to discover—in a world of things I couldn't do—something I *could* do. Even at that tender age, I knew I wanted to help others succeed. I might not have been the sharpest tool in the woodshed, but I did learn I was good at helping others. My second-grade teacher and my principal gave definition to my young life when they said, "You have been chosen to help the first graders get started in the second grade." I am a helper today. That is what my life has been about, and it all began in the second grade...my second time around.

Recess Is Over

But even with extra attention, school didn't get any easier. I remember standing at the blackboard one day in the fourth grade, trying desperately to solve a long-division problem. The numbers just didn't make sense to me. The longer I stood there, the more difficult it became, until finally my teacher's frustration got the best of her. With some indignation she instructed me to stand there until I got the right answer.

Thankfully it was late in the class period, or I would have been standing at the board for the entire day. I couldn't multiply *or* divide numbers. Dyscalcula causes a short circuit in that part of your brain, and numbers tend to all run together. As I sit here writing this, I admit I *still* struggle with basic multiplication tables (although I've gotten pretty good with fives, if you give me a minute).

When I was growing up, diagnosticians didn't know much about different learning modalities or how to diagnose learning disabilities. All I knew was that I was having trouble getting through school, and I was sure that fourth grade was going to be the last grade I ever passed.

It wasn't. But it *did* mark the first of the final three years I would enjoy summer break. Starting in the seventh grade, I began going to school year-round, just trying to keep up with my schoolwork until graduation.

Math remained a mystery. I failed algebra as many times as you can take it, each time feeling like more of a failure. Most of my friends were doing well in school, while I was spending all year there, yet *still* falling behind. I felt like the village idiot.

Sometime during the fourth grade, my mom and dad started fighting more. I had always wanted to be close to my dad and, in some ways, felt that I was. I loved the outdoors and would have lived in the woods if allowed. I hunted, fished, worked cattle with my granddad, and spent as much time as I could with both my grandparents, whom I adored.

Home, however, was not a happy place. I was afraid of my mother, who frequently slapped me and did a lot of yelling when I was around.

One day it all boiled over. Although I can't even remember the specifics now, my brother, Jim, and I did something, and it must have been *bad*. When my dad got home, he began yelling at my mother, and their argument got louder and quickly turned on Jim and me. We were dragged into the hallway, the doors to the bedrooms were closed, and Dad took off his belt and began to beat me. Jim, who was two years younger, was sobbing and trying to find a place to hide from it all. He was terrified.

Then it was his turn. I must have said something, because my dad turned back around to me, and the beating started all over again. That was the first time that I experienced being beaten unconscious, but it wouldn't be the last. One moment I was lying on the floor looking at my dad's shoes as he was standing next to me. Next I woke up in bed.

I cried that night like I never had before. My life had changed because my concept of my dad had changed. I stopped trying to get close to my father or to see him as a friend. He was someone who would hurt me if he wanted to, and I was now afraid of him.

Bruises of the Heart

In town our family was respected and well liked. My parents were active in church and civic groups, and they participated in school events, which created some internal confusion for me. If *they* weren't the problem, I thought, then *I* must be. After a while, I started to believe the regular blowups were probably all my fault and that I just needed to learn how to behave.

When I got to the sixth grade, I was allowed a few more privileges. I could ride my bicycle to go to the swimming pool or play golf. One day I came home after a day of fun, and the minute I walked in the door, my mother slapped me and began to scream at me. I was clueless as to what she was angry about or what I might have done. I was home early, and I hadn't gone anywhere I wasn't permitted to go. She said, "When your dad gets home, *you're going to get it!*" I felt confusion and panic rising up inside me.

And then he came home.

The usual place for spankings was in the hallway, so that's where I went. I remember the beating that day more clearly than any other, because I didn't know what it was for. After it was all over, my mother glared at me and told me never to embarrass them again. I still didn't know what I had done.

"You *knew* someone would say something about the marks on your back, didn't you?" she accused. "What marks?" I wondered. I had no idea what she was talking about until I went to my room and looked in the mirror. There they were—bruises from a spanking I had gotten a week or so before. Apparently someone at the pool had seen them, called my mother out of concern, and asked if she could help. I never went to the pool again without checking my back first.

I grew to hate being at home and spent all of my free time away with friends, whose parents treated me like part of their families. I never told anyone what was going on in my home, although I came close to telling one afternoon when my friends Joe and Jim came by to pick me up after a particularly rough morning. I lay down in the backseat of the car and just cried. Being boys, they didn't ask, so I didn't tell. I was glad they were there for me in that way, but we didn't talk about feelings. It never occurred to us that it might be a good thing to do.

No one would have guessed that all was not well in our home. I wouldn't know where to start if I was to try to share some of my pain, anyway. And what would happen if someone *did* believe me? Would I have to live with someone else and break any contact with my grandparents? I grew to hate that part of my life and, looking back, see it only as overwhelmingly sad.

I learned to hide my true feelings and became good at putting on a happy face, no matter what was going on around me. I also wanted desperately for others to like me.

Similar Experiences, Different Constraints

During this time two core beliefs formed in my heart and mind. First, I deeply believed that *no one would ever really love me,* and the second belief, which was even more hurtful, was the reason that no one would ever really love me: I was convinced *I was unlovable.* Somehow, something was wrong with me that made it impossible for others to love me. That painful thought continued with me well into adulthood.

Sadly, the core belief of being unlovable is one that many children develop and is incredibly difficult to overcome. What's worse, it's the catalyst for many personal constraints. It can easily turn to anger and high aggression—anger toward those who are supposed to be there for you but aren't, and aggression toward anyone who lets you down because they are treading on wounds first opened by parents or other "trusted" authorities.

Others struggle with resulting identity issues and a sense of needing to perform. Performance was a big constraint for me. I tried to please people by doing more and by performing better, which often meant—as an adult—doing things for everyone else at the expense of doing what was right for my family or myself. This core belief can also lead to perfectionism, overcompensation, and even procrastination, all driven by the need to be blameless and to gain the approval of others. Because of my learning disabilities and other shortcomings, I was determined to do well in Scouts, baseball, and other sports. Although I appeared to be doing well, much of the motivation for my activities was overcompensation for feeling horribly inadequate at school. Yet I never felt I was getting very far. It seemed like I was always trying to catch up just to break even.

Another constraint that can come from feeling unloved is that a person can become overly nurturing toward others with the hope that it will be reciprocated. This is a serious problem for many women who are natural "givers" as they seek desperately to receive the depth of affection they give out. Many young women are especially prone to getting into relationships with people who need rescuing in some way. Since they are emotionally unhealthy, these relationships help them feel needed and—by extension—loved. But, unfortunately, "givers" generally attract "takers," who leave the high-nurturing person feeling as though he or she has been exploited and used. Once they are able to recognize their own part in setting up this unhealthy dynamic, they can learn to spot the warning signs before the damage occurs.

I became an overperformer and an overnurturer. During this painful time of transition and growth, I had to learn how to love what I did for its own rewards rather than needing someone's approval. It was also a challenge to be able to love unconditionally, without having internal "demands" that I be loved back.

Healing Is a Choice

Shortly after deciding to write this book, I wanted to know if my picture of our childhood and perceptions of events was accurate. I called my brother Jim, and he agreed to come over. We sat in my backyard next to the lake and compared notes on our years at home, including some of our most painful memories. Finally, I asked him why Dad never beat him like he did me.

Without even looking up, he said, "That's easy. It's your own fault that Dad beat you like he did. You were afraid of him, and I wasn't."

Then Jim looked me square in the eyes. "I told him I would kill him if he ever beat me again."

My brother is a good man, but he was hurt by our parents just as deeply as I was. His resulting constraints, however, were different from mine. Instead of performance and nurturance issues, his issues were with anger and aggression. He also became defensive. Today he is a successful businessman, but he, like me and so many others, had to work hard to overcome some of the things that impacted us as boys. That day it was good to sit and discuss our childhood to see how we had each dealt with things differently, yet successfully.

Many years after I had become an adult, I went home for my annual visit. My parents had divorced, and both were living alone. I went to see my dad. I had already decided that when I got out of the car, I would not shake his hand as he always wanted, but I would hug and hold him. As he walked up with his hand held out and my family getting out of the car behind me, I hugged him. After what seemed like an eternity, I stepped back and told him that I loved him, then I hugged him again.

He had been standing there with his hand stuck out for a handshake, and on the second hug, he put his head on my shoulder and cried.

Late that night the two of us sat in the living room alone. I shared with him how much I had been hurt and how much I had wanted him to love me. I looked over at my dad sitting in the chair next to me. He had his head down, and tears were falling quietly to the floor.

That night I forgave my dad. We cried together, and we both became whole. A few years later I was lying in his bed at home, cradling him in my arms like a child, while he was dying of cancer. I am so thankful I had the opportunity to forgive and to overcome those early hurts in my life.

During the same time period, I got a call from my mother. Mom asked if my wife, Susan, and I could come to Houston to see her. Although I lived less than two hours away, I saw her only once a year. We took her to a nice restaurant for dinner, and as the waiter left with our orders, Mother looked across the table with tears running down her face.

She softly said, "I want to tell you why we never loved you."

Susan, being a great wife, was patting my knee under the table as I responded, "I know why, Mom. It's not necessary for you to talk about it."

But she needed to unburden her heart. She went on to tell the story about how she became pregnant and how this had directed much of their own frustration and anger toward me, which was why she had acted like she had when I was young. It broke my heart to see her go through the telling of the story she had hidden all of her life. Her sense of shame was immense, yet it was incredibly freeing for her to share her pain with us. I held her hand and said, "That's all gone now, Mom. We have the future." And we did, for another five years, until she passed away as well.

Personal constraints are just that. They are personal, and they constrain you in many ways. Some are from birth, others from your childhood experiences, and still others you pick up—like dangerous hitchhikers—along life's unpredictable road. But no matter where your personal constraints come from, they all have one thing in common: unless you can find and remove them, they will certainly hold you back from your greatest plans, hopes, and aspirations in life.

17 Personal-Constraint Combinations

Marriage is supposed to be the ultimate partnership.

We get married so we can spend the rest of our lives with another person. In marriage we also become legal business partners. We have the opportunity to raise kids together; to make decisions together; to buy and sell together; to invest, save, plan, and share everything there is in life to share—together.

But there is more. Marriage is also the ultimate combining of personal constraints. When I married Susan I also married her personal constraints—and what's worse, she married mine.

My constraints married her constraints.

Let me tell you, that combination had better work. If we both struggle with low self-control, we are probably in trouble. If I have high drive and passion and she scores very low on drive and passion, we will probably have conflicts over my desire to do more with my life and her need to be satisfied with me coming home at five every day.

Fortunately (or perhaps because we both knew what we wanted), I have the best possible partnership with my wife I could ever hope to have. Our personal constraints are synergistic. For example, her strong organizational skills work for both of us, despite my own tendencies toward disorganization. Yet I am much more entrepreneurial, and risk taking comes easier to me, which allows me to move faster and think more globally than she does. My self-control scales are lower than Susan's; she is more reflective and needs more information to make decisions than I do. Those behavioral attributes work for us for two reasons. First, our strengths and personal constraints are well balanced, and second, we both recognize the value the other brings and have a desire to listen and learn from each other. Can you imagine what life would be like if we were both highly dominant, with a need to be in control of everything?

The same principles hold true for the combination of constraints that exist within a person as well. Some combinations work well, and others are disastrous. The difference between "winners" and "losers" in life can often be found in the various combinations of constraints.

For example, what happens if you have high aggression and great social skills? You will be very competitive but great with people as well. That's a good combination. You might have the potential to be a great salesman or a world-class athlete or coach. For that matter this combination can generate a valuable employee—someone who's competitive and has a desire to succeed at everything he or she does. Because that person would also have the social skills needed to be successful, we can easily see him or her doing well in many areas of life.

But what if we drop just one trait from that makeup? What if we take away the nurturing aspect of great social skills? What would we expect then? We could easily have someone like Ivan Boesky, the Wall Street trader who scammed hundreds of senior citizens—primarily women—out of their life savings while smiling the whole time. His great social skills put people at ease, but his high aggression and low nurturing caused him to reach his own goals at the expense of others.

Our personal constraints always play themselves out in the systems in which we operate. When the combinations of constraints are in the killer constraint area, you will find some deeply damaging behaviors.

Let me talk about a particular issue that tells a lot about how visible someone's other constraints are: low self-control. Dr. Chris

White, my coauthor and head of our assessment and coaching group, likes to say that low self-control is an amplifier.

If a person has a combination of high aggression and low self-control, then the low self-control is an amplifier. The high aggression is unleashed through the low self-control. Therefore, the high aggression is acted out and becomes a problem. In effect low self-control amplifies the high aggression. It's not a good combination to have.

On the other hand high aggression and high self-control combined looks quite different. High self-control is a masker. It covers up the high aggression so it is not easily seen by others.

As you think through the combinations of constraints, let's also consider the effect of the amplifier. In addition some of the biggest killer combinations follow.

Volcano/Quick Draw

The types of behaviors you will see acted out are: anger, impatience, yelling, criticisms, sarcasm, storming off from arguments, cussing, name-calling, and other overtly aggressive actions. This is the typical Mike Tyson profile that we often see acted out in sports and other areas. Mike occasionally puts on exhibition fights in Las Vegas, and recently during a workout, he was asked if he would ever fight professionally again. His answer may tell us more about what is going on inside him than anything that has ever been written about him. He simply said, "To get in the ring and fight professionally, I have to become that other person. I don't like that person, and I don't ever want to become him again." Profoundly insightful and perhaps the most healing decision he could ever make. I'm pulling for him to get better each day.

Action Rx:

If you have this combination, you will have to learn something that you should have learned in elementary school. Be quiet!!!! Keeping your mouth shut is a good thing. While you are learning to do this, you might also consider letting the people you get in the most conflict with (spouse, others) know that you will need to take some breaks but that the purpose of the break is to get good control over your emotions so that you can come back and finish the discussion in a more appropriate manner. Let the other person also know that this is something that you are working on so that they aren't standing there thinking that they are the source of the problem, when the real sources are your low self-control and anger.

I know that in some ways this sounds harsh, but for tough people who are strong willed, this is all right. You know what needs to be done, and you have the ability to do it. You simply have to have a plan. Learn to take a break from the conflict, go for a short walk, sit outside for a minute, get quiet, and think about this: "What is my goal at this moment?" If your goal is to hurt the other person either verbally or physically, then you have to own up to that and think through what you are really saying. Is that really what you want? Or do you simply want them to listen and do what you are saying? You need to consider what you are saying. If you want to be loved or listened to, then you have to be someone that others would want to hear and love. Blowing up and bullying others will not ever get you respect and love. It will get you rejected, over and over and over. Make a change today. Go for a walk, get still, and apologize often. It works, and you will be better for it.

Marshmallow/Ostrich

I see this combination in many fine people. They tend to be caring, loving individuals who are always tending to others. However, the low self-confidence also means that they can be easily taken advantage of because they don't see their own value. One of our staff members, Frances, is a high-nurturing person who struggled with low self-confidence for years. We watched her former employer take advantage of this combination time and time again. After twelve years of never getting a raise although she continued to be a star performer, she met with us to discuss joining our company. We were thrilled to have her and quickly offered her a job. She is incredible, but we can't be the only ones who recognize and value that; Frances has to recognize and value it also. Because she has learned to do this, today she is a very different person.

This combination also shows up frequently in family dynamics. Often the mom will take care of everything with little help from others; yet she won't ask for help because she really believes that she should be taking care of everything. Her job is to make everyone else happy. Mom needs more balance and higher self-confidence so she can take better care of herself in the process.

Action Rx:

Self-confidence is an interesting concept. To improve your sense of self-confidence, first, you need to know that your picture of yourself is not the complete picture. When your self-confidence is low, you will notice that you tend to focus on the negatives in your life much more than the positives. Even as you read this, you may be thinking, "If there were positives I would think about them." But that's not really true. The odds are good that you have lost sight of all the positives in your life because your vision is clouded by the negatives that keep popping up in front of you. Identify some things that you do well. Write them down and put them in a prominent place, such as on your desk or your mirror. What is something special about you that you do really well? Is it being a true and loyal friend? Is there something that you do at work that is especially good? Perhaps you excel as a mother, father, or spouse or perhaps you are good with animals.

In children you can see self-confidence as it grows. When children see that they can do something, they have an increased sense of self-confidence. Watch a boy throw a rock farther than he did before and notice how much taller he carries himself. The same is true for girls as well. And guess what? The same is true for adults. When we see that we do something well, we grow in self-confidence. Don't let the negatives in your life taunt you to the point that you can't see the gifts you possess.

Bulldozer/Volcano

This is a tough combination and is almost always explosive. These people tend to run over everyone around them, abusing them in the process. If the scales are extremely high, it's not enough to dominate others, they have to virtually destroy them in the process.

If, however, the high dominance and high aggression is coupled with the amplifier of low self-control, then you have someone who is easily recognized because they really are overpowering. Although these people can do well in business, they usually struggle with relationships in their personal life. The negative aspects of their behaviors play themselves out in their professional lives as well, usually indicated by high employee-turnover rates. People at the very high end of these scales are easy to spot. They tend to congregate with others who are like them—in prison. At a younger age we would easily identify them as bullies. Unless they deal with these behaviors, their prognosis for long-term success is quite low.

Action Rx:

Bulldozers and volcanoes are interesting people. They blow up quickly and don't back down very often. If you are struggling with this combination, these thoughts will be helpful for you. First, you need to know that this has been part of your makeup for a long time. It didn't just happen yesterday, and other people didn't cause you to be this way. This is an issue, and it's your issue. So let's deal with it.

First, quit pushing on everyone. Let others have some say in things. You are not always right even though you think you are. If you want to be right about something, then be right about how you treat others rather than trying to be right by being the authority. Let's set a goal that you will work at being the "authority" on being thoughtful and considerate. Listening is not a strong suit for you, and this will need to be an area in which you make a special effort.

Now let's think about what happens when the volcano part kicks in. You will need to consider walking away and letting the other person know that you will come back in a short while. If you are in a business meeting, you will really need to think about sitting back and being quiet. I have a great friend who began doing this during his executive team meetings. There was a person on the team who really got in his face about things, and it was difficult for him to do, but he learned how to sit back in his chair rather than lean in and appear intense. It would also be good to realize that you really lose influence with others if you are constantly "going off" on them or others in meetings. If you want to be influential, then exercise more control over your actions.

Finally, when you do blow it, go back and apologize to the person or team you were with when you exploded. When you apologize be sure to ask for forgiveness rather than simply saying, "I'm sorry." Make it a statement that they have the chance to respond to. This will also go a long way toward helping you learn that you don't want to continue acting that way.

Bulletproof/Turtle

This is an interesting combination. Recently I was speaking at a large conference with thousands of people in attendance. A young lady had been asked to sing during the opening for the conference. She was seventeen years old, and I have rarely heard anyone her age with her level of talent. I wasn't surprised that she had been asked to sing for the group, and I knew they were in for a treat. Then I saw her practice on stage and couldn't have been more disappointed. She looked great, and her voice was amazing, but she didn't move. She just stood there. She stood in one place and didn't move her hands or smile or even open her eyes during her whole rehearsal. The contradiction was striking. I was watching someone who looked dead with the most alive voice I could imagine.

Then came the hard part. Her chaperone came over to me and said, "We are hoping that you will take a few minutes and give her some feedback on how she can be better. She doesn't listen to us, and we're hoping that she will listen to you."

Oh, boy. Here we go. After she walked off the stage, she sat down next to me and said, "I love that song, and I think it will make all the difference tomorrow, don't you?"

That was the opening I needed. I said, "It was great. The song is right, and your voice is perfect for it. Could I offer some suggestions for presenting to a crowd this large that might be helpful?"

She looked at me and said, "Sure, I guess."

I suggested that she might open her eyes and make eye contact with her audience and that she needed to move around the stage more for greater presence. I also suggested that using her hands during her song would better emphasize the points that she was trying to make. Now keep in mind that she was seventeen years old and had never sung to an audience this large before. It would have been understandable if she felt a little overwhelmed or frightened by the size of the auditorium. Not her. Her self-confidence was very high, and her Turtle mentality was in full swing. She looked at me with the most sincere smile and said, "My voice will carry the moment. It's very good and that's what I'm here for—to sing. I'm not an entertainer. I'm a singer. My voice is fine, and I'm sorry that you can't appreciate that for what it is." Whoa. I thought I had picked up a rattlesnake. Kindly, I suggested again that her performance would have much more impact if she used her hands and connected with her audience some during her song. "I have always done it this way, and I wouldn't be here if I wasn't good—would I?" She was not being aggressive or hostile, just highly self-confident. Later that night her agent said that they had the same problem with her, and they had hoped that she would listen to me.

The next day came quickly, as the night ended late. The opening event took place with a very talented young man engaging the audience. Instantly everyone was on their feet and enjoying the moment, as he had them all singing along with him. WOW, what a start to an education event. The pace was fast, and more introductions were made, and then the young lady took the stage and began her song. You could instantly feel the momentum cut short. And then it happened. Perhaps one hundred or more people decided this was an opportunity to take a break. Her voice was great, but with no stage presence and no effort made to engage the audience, she found no connection. Without a connection, they had no reason to stay.

I thought that she would be hurt by the reaction of the audience, but quite the contrary. Following her performance and the lackluster response of the crowd, her comment to me was that the program was poorly put together, and everyone should have had a break after the first forty-five minutes. That was her opinion, even though in all of her seventeen years, she had never been to a professional conference and had no basis for her observation other than the fact that the audience didn't respond the way she thought they should. The issue wasn't the way the program was put together. It was her unwillingness to change, compounded by her high self-confidence.

Action Rx:

In order for her to get better, our young singer would have to want and receive honest feedback. Herein is the problem. With her Bulletproof thinking she is unlikely to get there easily. Most likely some painful events will jolt her enough to make her listen to someone. I know that if her agent asks me to recommend her to others, I will respectfully decline. But that won't be enough. There will need to be something that is seriously jolting to her, again because of her high self-confidence. Once that "jolt" happens, then she will be in a spot where she can hear some feedback. This is one of those constraints that so gets in the way of personal growth that it is almost impossible to break through it with a simple discussion. Events have a way of ultimately bringing reality home to a person, and the process is usually painful.

We are all complex creatures, and you can't oversimplify the factors that contribute to who we are. The way I see it, it's not in the "who we are" but the "who we can be" that I find my greatest hope.

Critic/Flatliner

Let's look at another combination that is interesting. Critics are those people who are never happy with anything. They complain and generally are the naysayers of any group. Critics are hard on people and difficult to be around; children avoid them, and adults often "forget" to include them for parties or other social events where "fun" is on the agenda.

Flatliners are people who have very low drive—one has to check their pulse periodically just to make sure they're still alive and functioning! Flatliners don't engage in life or make things happen—in fact, they almost get tired just *watching* things happen. Can you imagine what a Flatliner Critic would look like? Actually, it's not that hard—two words describe this combo: Archie Bunker.

A few years ago I was on a trip with a friend, and we made plans to visit one of his acquaintances for the weekend. As we arrived my friend's friend was angrily screaming at one of his kids. I felt awkward as I got out of the car and stepped right into the scenario. Not him. He seemed perfectly comfortable with raging at his son in the front yard. He didn't stop to speak or wave or introduce himself to me or welcome his friend, who was with me. He simply walked around to the backyard. "Great," I thought, "I've got a weekend of this to look forward to."

When we walked into the house, his wife couldn't have been more pleasant. She welcomed us warmly, with a big smile and a lot of activity in the kitchen as she was preparing a mouthwatering feast for our dinner. What a contrast! Then the Critic showed up again.

His first words were "When is supper going to be ready?" Finally he came over and spoke a few words to his friend and introduced himself to me. I was secretly hoping that he was about to say that he'd forgotten to tell us he already had plans for the weekend and had to leave immediately.

The next forty-eight hours with this guy lived up to the previews. He made everyone around him miserable. We went fishing on a gorgeous lake in gorgeous weather, and he complained. We caught fish, but they were "not as good as last time." His wife was a great cook, and we ate well, "but it was not like her *last* pecan pie." We had fun with his kids, but "they're stupid," he let us know. Nothing was right for this guy. From the moment we got out of the car to the time we got back in to leave, he found something to gripe about.

He told us about his job, which consisted of sitting and watching dials all day. Some guys can do that kind of work and take pride in what they are asked to do. But not our Archie, no sir. He reads novels and magazines. "If something goes wrong at the plant, the bells and lights will go off and tell me. I don't have to sit there all day like an idiot and watch those dials." His words pretty much summed up his attitude toward his job, and he made several statements about how he'd be sure management didn't take advantage of *him*. He had been doing the same thing for twelve years. His Flatliner attributes kept him from moving, even though his Critic side kept him from enjoying his work.

His wife carried the load at home and at work. It was obvious that she was the one with the drive and the talent in the family. His kids avoided him like a disease, and actually he *was* a carrier of a life-killing virus called criticalness. Nothing was right for him. Nothing worked around him. Everything was wrong, and he was going to tell you about it. Mind you, he wasn't going to *do* anything about it—he was simply going to point it out in case you hadn't noticed how bad it was.

The female version is just as difficult. I have seen many women over the years fall into this trap over time as they become more disillusioned with their life. In some cases opportunities to grow and be fulfilled in life have bypassed them—they never worked outside the home, or they took a job they didn't like simply because they needed to make an income. As their children grow older, their roles begin to change, and they can no longer hide behind the busyness and responsibilities of being "Mom." Becoming more disenchanted with their own life, all they see are others having more fun or accomplishing dreams and plans—and resentment builds. With time bitterness sets in and begins to cloud their everyday experiences. They become chronic complainers with little sense of significance in their life, and this affects all their relationships. One day they wake up and find that they have become Critics and Flatliners—people with little meaning or direction in their life, yet believing they are unable to change.

They didn't start out that way. It just happened over time, and before they knew it, their unhappiness turned them into people others find it difficult to be around. Not a good place to find yourself at the end of twenty years.

I confess to my humanity: I am like most other people when it comes to being around people like this. I would rather not be around them. They hurt people by being so negative and difficult. They are especially hard on children, and it's not fun to watch. If you try to intervene, you usually end up drowning in their whirlpool of issues.

Action Rx:

First, if you are like this—*you need to change.* Think about Archie Bunker. He had a great family, yet all he could do was complain. He was content to constantly belittle and mock others for any weakness he could dream up. Do *you* want to be in Archie's camp, never realizing how others view you and your harsh ways? Do you really get satisfaction from being this way?

Second, you need to apologize. You have hurt those around you, and you have let them down. I watched a very close relative of mine do this. Fortunately, he finally saw the destruction he was causing and decided to change. He went humbly to his wife and asked her for forgiveness. He did the same thing with his daughters—he asked them to forgive him, and they cried. Then, for the first time in his life, *he* cried. He cried for all the pain he had caused them and all the time he had lost when he might have been living a meaningful life. It was a powerful time of reconnection and healing.

But it didn't stop there. He made a commitment to change, and he asked for assistance. I helped direct the process, and we all agreed that every time he started back into his old habits, his family would call him on it. If he started complaining about something or someone, they would look at him and say, "Does this work for you?" which was his cue to change his approach and his words. For the first few weeks, it was a comedy routine. He couldn't believe how much he complained. Over time he went through being frustrated to being angry to becoming a better man. It took two years for him to get where he wanted to be.

The Flatliner part of the equation creates challenges in executing the process of change. At home Flatliners often tell everyone what to do, but they don't do it themselves. They are so used to underperforming that it is built into their routines. They don't help with the dishes, they don't help with the kids, they don't help with projects—they just flat don't help. When they *do* decide to pitch in and do something, they get it only halfway done, and even then it's late.

Look around you. Instead of seeing what everyone else can do better, decide on something that needs doing—and just do it. You'll be surprised at the difference it makes.

If you are a woman who has been raising kids and now find more time on your hands, realize the gift of time you have earned and redeem it. Don't wait for someone to call you—*you* make the call. Recently, a lady was complaining to me about her struggle with loneliness and boredom, and I asked her what she had done to make things different. She immediately responded, "No one has any time to help me get started." Wrong attitude. It's your life—you must take the initiative to do something with it. If you need help getting started, make some calls until you find a place to offer your talents. Believe me, lots of things need doing in the world. Just find one, and you will find fulfillment.

You can make a difference. However, the first difference you need to make is in yourself. It's a great place to begin...and you don't even have to leave home to get started on that project.

18 OPC Starts at Home

My work over the years has focused greatly on assisting companies and schools to use the principles of OPC to help employees and students identify and overcome their greatest barriers to achievement.

But the opportunity to lay the best foundation for OPC starts at home. Why? Because there is no place where our constraints are more obvious than at home. If I have problems with anger at work, you can bet they will be multiplied many times over at home. The constraints that we fail to address in life will play themselves out at home regardless of how well we are able to hide them in public. And some hidden constraints are the most devastating when they surface in situations that involve family members or those most important to us.

We are more of who we are when we are at home than anywhere else. My wife, Susan, has often pointed out various behaviors to me, saying, "You would never do that in public," and I have to confess there is considerable truth to that comment. I spend most of my time being aware of how I need to act in public and realizing that everyone from my staff to our customers needs me to be appropriate and to model the principles of what I teach consistently. Home is where I relax.

But my constraints are most evident when I am with my family. Fortunately my wife provides a vital source of feedback. Susan's input is more than just an opinion to me—it is the compass that points me in the right direction and helps make me more of the person I need and want to be. She is always honest with me without any reservations, and it is that feedback—combined with her love and encouragement—that helps me grow. Married men have an advantage. It is little wonder that married men outlive single men, as we have all the advantages when it comes to doing well in life. This does not always appear to be the case when you consider the divorce rate and the high level of marital dissatisfaction expressed today. But the data is solidly in favor of marriage, and good marriages are not easily dismissed. It is in the daily exchanges of honest, intimate relationships that we truly grow.

The Gift of Change

When my first son was born, I did something that was perhaps the most important thing I have ever done as a parent and maybe as a man. The day that Matthew came home from the hospital, I got him all settled in and his mother taken care of.

I was so happy to finally have a child, but I was also acutely aware of the things in my life that would not work for me as a parent. I needed to change, and I knew it. That night after his mother had fallen asleep, I took him out of the crib and carried him to the backyard. There, under a beautiful Texas night sky, I sat in the grass with him and pulled his little shirt up and just looked at how small he was. Then I placed my hand on his chest and said, "Matthew, I commit to you that I will change everything in my life that I need to change so I can be the parent that you need me to be. I commit to do this so that you can fulfill the destiny that lies before you. I love you more than life itself."

After a while I took him back in the house and got out my journal. I wrote down what kind of man I wanted him to become. That was the easy part: a man of integrity with the courage to stand up for what he thought was right, a man of commitment and principles and someone who knew what it meant to stick by his word. I wanted him to have character and initiative and have the ability to make things happen rather than wait for someone to tell him what needed to be done. That list was easy.

The next list was tough. I wrote down the things that I needed to change so that he could become that kind of man. As a boy I had always stuffed my feelings down like lots of young boys do. As an adult I was struggling to learn how to express them. Sometimes they came out in angry words, and sometimes they didn't come out at all. But perhaps the biggest things I struggled with were my own insecurities. I couldn't stand to be wrong because that meant I wasn't very smart—and, therefore, was not acceptable. I would argue over ridiculous things, and I talked too much. I didn't listen to others when I really needed to hear what they had to say. I got along well with people and had good social skills; otherwise my own issues would have exposed me as an unwelcome guest, for sure. Add to that mix the fact that I was strong willed and intense . . . and it wasn't a good picture. I had to change (the list was longer, but that gives you an idea of what I was working with). I knew that if I chose to allow some of these constraints to remain in my life, Matthew would be heavily influenced by them—possibly even be doomed to repeat them—and that wasn't good enough for my son. I still have those lists today, and I think about them often. Thankfully the things I'm working on now aren't the same things I was working on then.

That was the commitment that I made to him, and I have repeated that same promise on each and every birthday he has had since that night. I have done the same thing with his brother, Micah, since the night he was born, and I have repeated the same commitment to each of the other children that we have raised, as well.

Last year, Matthew and his wife, Heather, and their children were at the house on his birthday. Later that night he and I went into our backyard, and I sat down next to him and reached over to pull him to me so that I could do the same thing that I have done for more than thirty years with my son. As I reached for him, he asked me, "Pop, how do you feel about the product of your labors?"

I lost it. I cried as I told him how proud I was of the parent, husband, and employer that he had become. Then, in that tender moment, he said, "I wasn't talking about me—you were the one who needed to change, weren't you?" We both laughed, and I wanted to smack him at the same time for teasing me, but it was a moment I'll remember.

What was the key in this whole process? I believe one of the greatest aspects was my realization that certain priorities are more important than others in our lives, and those priorities must get the attention they deserve. I also believe that if those most significant things *don't* get the attention they deserve, the resulting loss is potentially devastating.

Before Matthew came, I thought I was a fairly easygoing person. But I soon learned that I didn't like to wait on others, and when I was ready to go, *I was really ready to go.* This doesn't work with a one-year-old, nor does it work when children are ten years of age, or sixteen. I had plenty of time to come to the profound understanding that the world didn't revolve around me. I had to learn how to deal with my impatience and how to set my agenda aside so I could focus on the more important matter of Matthew's growth.

Let me give you an example. I like to come home and read the paper and relax for a few minutes before I help with supper and the dishes. But what do you do when you come home and the boys want to play catch? You play catch—that's what you do. And if you are reading the paper, you stop reading and go change clothes to play ball. What do you do when the boys are having an argument and they need to be corrected while you are reading the paper? You deal with the issue, and you manage your own temper in the process.

If you are a parent, you change. And if you don't change, then you aren't being a parent—you are still acting like you did when you were single, except that you now have kids who are behaving a lot like you. Many people don't deal with their kids appropriately because they refuse to deal with their own issues first. Selfish parents won't change the things that need to be changed in order to help give their kids a better start in life.

I knew my decisions would impact my family in many ways. The journey began with a promise between my boys and me. I needed to change, and specific character issues needed to be addressed—and I decided to get on with it.

Children have a way of exposing our constraints. We may go through much of life thinking we are really pretty well put together, but it takes only one child to show us how self-centered we really are. The problem is that they are selfish, too. As one dad told me, "I'm the adult. I should get my way first. I pay the bills—let him wait until *he* has money." Of course, after griping, he went ahead and did what he should have done for his son in the first place. The fact is that human beings are born selfish, and as we grow, we must have a reason to change. For me that reason was my sons. I would like to tell you that I changed for other reasons, such as my wife or my desire for personal growth. But it wasn't until the birth of my children that I realized that they depended on me for *everything* in their lives, and if I didn't get this child-raising thing right, they would be the ones who paid for it; they would pay for my parenting mistakes for the rest of their lives.

Off to the Mission with a Mission

Can social skills be taught? Of course they can. Every mother in the country is trying to teach her kids not to drink out of the milk carton and how to use a fork at the table. Social skills can be, and are, easily taught. Most of us learn these lessons early in life. By this I mean that we learn the basics: keeping your clothes on in public, chewing with your mouth closed, and not using your hands to pick up your mashed potatoes. Social skills are also essential for success in corporate life, and they will certainly differentiate between those who do well and those who don't.

Okay, so we *can* teach social skills. But can empathy and kindness be taught? The answer is yes and maybe. Although data is discouraging on empathy being taught to adults, it clearly *can* be taught to children, and it's essential to do so.

When my boys were ten and twelve, I told them that we would be taking a special field trip one Saturday in place of our weekly visit to the boys' ranch to work with our staff. Awakening at 6:30 a.m., we got ready and left for downtown Bryan, Texas. Parking the car several blocks from the city mission, I took a few moments to explain to them what we could expect as we visited the mission for the day. I told the boys that I would be getting them a meal there and that they were not to mention my name, as I was fairly well known around town. I would use my real first name, Menville—you can see why I don't go by it—and we would hope that they would feed us.

With my hat in my hand and my head bowed, I entered the door to the office of the mission and asked for food for my sons. The lady at the desk was kind and attentive without making us feel poor. She asked if I needed anything else, and I said, "Only that my sons have something to eat." She handed me meal tickets for all three of us. I thanked her, and we went and stood outside the cafeteria to wait until the doors opened for breakfast. The cafeteria was around the corner from the main part of the mission, which was in a poor area downtown, with several of the buildings nearby in great need of repair. The area immediately around the mission cafeteria was clean and well kept but had obviously been built many years earlier.

While we were standing there, a small group of people began to congregate at the door. They came from all walks of life, most of them noticeably poor and in ill health, as well. There were women who had been very drunk the night before and there were men who didn't know who they were. Most of them were not very clean and suffered from moderate to serious mental issues that affected their ability to function normally. One of the men was in his sixties, with a large nose and strong, rough hands that had known hard labor. He had a large, tumorlike growth on the back of his head, which added to his odd appearance. My youngest son, Micah, couldn't keep from staring at him. Matthew kept elbowing his brother, telling him to quit staring, but what can a ten-year-old do?

Eventually the doors opened and the group began to move inside the cafeteria. The tables around the room had benches at some and chairs at others. We stood in line and waited to be served. As we stood there the man who had opened the doors began to harshly shout orders about who went first and that we were to take our hats off, "unless we were raised in a barn." Then he said, "Let's pray." Boy, what a switch.

As we went through the line, the food looked good, and both boys were hungry. Micah got his plate and walked over to a table with a sign that read, "Reserved for Families." They were the only children in the room. As he set his plate down, the man who had barked orders and then prayed came over and said, loudly, "Do you look like a family? I don't see a mother. This is reserved." Micah looked humiliated. He picked up his tray and went to find another spot to sit. The only one left was right next to the man with the big nose and the tumor on his head. The man offered Micah a seat next to him and then offered to cut his meat if he needed help. They talked to each other while Matthew and I sat across from them and visited with the other men. A deeper understanding took place that day in both of the boys.

We hung around for a few hours after breakfast, talking with different people; then we walked down the street, enjoying the sunshine, and sat down on the curb. I asked my sons, "What did you learn today?"

I will never forget the answer Micah gave me as his eyes widened. "Daddy, I never saw you without power before. You are always in charge of things, and today you weren't, and it scared me. You stood there with your hat in your hands and begged a meal for us."

Matthew saw some things, too. He said, "Daddy, what happened to get those people there? Why are they there? Lots of them look like they really have problems."

The Seeds of Change

And then we talked. Were they bad people or did they just have some really tough things happen to them? We talked about what it is like to lose a job and not be able to find another one and what it would be like to have to feed your sons if you didn't have a job and couldn't get one. We talked about the Depression, when most people lost everything and, yes, that it could happen again. The boys learned that hard lives don't make people bad at all, and we agreed that the man with the tumor was really nice, even though at first he looked a little scary. Most important, the "million-dollar question" came up later in the discussion:

Could we help them in some way?

Empathy was made real to my sons that day. They learned that caring was a start, but it had to have behavior attached to it or it was just words. They were deeply touched that day, and each of them was better for the experience. For some people these feelings are difficult to develop because they have never been able to identify with another person's pain. For various reasons they have closed themselves off from emotions and remain distant from others. This happens most frequently when a young person is not bonded to another person early in life or when they are traumatized early on and become unable to feel concern for anyone but themselves. If you don't feel connected to other people, then it is difficult to feel someone else's pain or emotions.

But too much empathy can present its own problems. When parents have empathy that is not balanced by other attributes, they will be too permissive with children. You will hear highly empathetic/nurturing parents saying things such as "Isn't that cute? Boys will be boys. Aren't they active? They sure are energetic, aren't they?" when most of these statements are cover-ups for inappropriate behaviors that aren't cute, boyish, active, or energetic. They are often budding character issues that go unaddressed but will, unfortunately, play out negatively in the child's social interactions.

Every day highly empathetic/nurturing parents negotiate with their kids in grocery stores and malls, and almost every time, the child walks out with a prize and reinforcement for this emerging constraint. *No* doesn't mean *no* any more than *stop* means *stop*. Words don't have meaning to overly empathetic parents; they use them without consequence, and at some point the child stops responding to the barrage of meaningless words and threats that fly about in the home.

Tantrums from the Playground
to the Boardroom

Not surprisingly one of the most frequently occurring constraints at home is anger. Where does this come from? How is it that we continue to struggle with anger and our tempers as adults when we should have dealt with this as adolescents? Where do these issues come from, and why do they stay with us into adulthood?

Age-appropriate issues must be addressed at various stages of life. For example, I expect all of my staff to be potty trained when they come to work. It would not be a good thing if they weren't. We don't ask about this during interviews, and I have never felt compelled to do so. This is an issue that is dealt with during an earlier stage of life (I hope). But what happens when issues that are age appropriate *don't* get dealt with during that age-appropriate period? *Issues don't go away simply because we get older.* They stay with us, often becoming more toxic with age, until we do something about them. Sometimes we learn to hide certain issues and live with them for years, but eventually any issues that we have not dealt with will show up. This is particularly the case with anger. Anger does not go away; it lies dormant and then blows up at the most inopportune times.

The unfortunate thing about people losing their temper is that quite often it works. It's much like the kid who doesn't want to do his schoolwork, and the next thing you know, he is fighting with the teacher and gets sent to the principal's office. His ploy worked!

It worked in school just like it worked at home. He threw a fit, a fight ensued, and he got sent to his room instead of having to finish the dishes. Again anger worked for him. It doesn't take long for kids to learn that they can get out of all kinds of things by throwing a screaming, yelling, bug-eyed, vein-popping, muscle-flexing fit. Then when they become adults, they simply continue to do what has always worked for them. I'm sure you can think of a boss or coworker or perhaps relative who controlled meetings or other people through intimidation or a reputation for angry blowups.

I expect kids to throw fits. They should throw fits. *Life is tough, and I don't like what is happening to me. I was in this really nice, cozy womb minding my own business, and the next thing I know some doctor is dragging me out with forceps, holding me upside down, slapping me, and passing me around the room.*

Why should kids be happy? And then to add insult to injury, we expect them to pick up their clothes, put away their dishes, feed the dog, and carry out the trash before they are allowed to watch their favorite cartoons.

This parenting thing is tough, and we don't get any do overs, so we'd better get it right. But what happens when parents *don't* get it right and the kid grows up throwing fits and learning that people will respond exactly as he wants them to—backing off and leaving him alone or scrambling around trying to make him happy? The bigger he gets, the bigger the problem gets. It's much easier on everyone involved to address anger when it is in diapers than to wait until it has matured into domestic abuse, road rage, or crimes of passion.

Developing Lifelong Habits

Financial issues are one of the top three marital battlegrounds (along with sex and balancing job/family demands, according to the

Center for Marriage and Family Research), yet we often overlook the importance of helping children learn how to handle money while they are young.

One of our sons, John, did what all young men seem to do when they get an after-school job. He burned through his money. John didn't give much thought to his future or how he was spending his paychecks. He was doing well in school, but when it came to finances, he spent every penny he earned.

John bought a truck and then began to fix it up with every addition known to man. He built a "boom box" for the backseat that took up the whole space and added ground effects. Then he installed a stereo—one that would have powered most small cities! At the end of the summer, he had no money, and when I asked him what he had done with his earnings, he said, "I don't know. I don't have much to show for it." Good for him. He was seeing something.

"What is the constraint that is affecting your finances?" I asked. After much thought he decided that it was his impulsiveness in making decisions, which was affecting his life in lots of areas. I challenged him, "John, can you come up with a way to change this so that it doesn't keep holding you back?"

His answer was a good one. "Yep, I can."

A plan was born that day to help him learn how to control this personal constraint. John agreed that he would not make any impulsive purchases and that he would set aside a certain percentage of each paycheck for savings. The plan was simple but has had a profound effect on him and his future.

Six months later we had another money talk—but this time about what he might do with the forty-five hundred dollars he had saved. A sense of pride in his self-control and an excited vision for his future replaced a vague, "I don't know where I'm going" attitude. He also said, smiling, "I don't want my friends to know how much money I have—because they'll want to borrow some of it!"

One less personal constraint for John—and over a lifetime, perhaps hundreds of thousands of dollars because of it. Unfortunately many people refuse to address the constraint of financial impulsiveness. Until they stop avoiding that hard but necessary work, they will never succeed to the fullest extent. They will remain stuck where they have always been, while others like John who have addressed this constraint move ahead. So where are you? Are you stuck, or are you moving forward?

19 OPC in the Workplace

In the previous chapter we talked about the impact of personal constraints at home and what can be done about them. But, as you know, they don't stop there. Our personal constraints go everywhere with us even though they often have more impact in one area than another. I think they are especially interesting in the business world. Our research has found solid patterns about different groups of businesspeople.

Entrepreneurs are an interesting bunch. I do not say that out of any personal conceit, since I see myself as an entrepreneur, but from having met so many fascinating, risk-taking, go-getting entrepreneurs over the years. I have also raised sons who are classic entrepreneurs, and they are the most interesting people you'd want to be around.

Entrepreneurs come equipped with basic character traits that can make or break them. For instance most are optimistic. If they weren't, they wouldn't believe in their own ideas enough to move forward with them. When they latch on to a good idea, they are positive they can—and will—succeed. They plunge ahead even when the funding is short and they have to move forward at great personal sacrifice.

Entrepreneur Profiles

Similarly entrepreneurs don't lack for confidence. I recall a young fellow who just *knew* that he could build and operate a bungee-jumping tower, even though he had never before built a tower or run a company. But Jake loved bungee jumping, and he really wanted to start his own company. He raised the funds, constructed his tower, and took the first jump. The bad news was that his bungee cord was too long—his overconfidence had jumped ahead of his research abilities. The good news was that he jumped over the Guadalupe River in Texas. Jake didn't drown, but he saw more fish than he wanted.

Overconfidence can convince people that they are able to accomplish anything—whether or not they have any prior experience in that area. But overconfidence becomes a major problem when it is paired with other constraints. High optimism and high self-confidence would describe most entrepreneur types. But what if low endurance is added to the mix?

Low-endurance entrepreneurs are not able to stay with a project when decision making needs focused attention. Instead this entrepreneur constantly angles for the next deal. He delegates the business operations to someone else, which is a nice way of saying that he loses interest in the day-to-day operations of the company. The easiest way to tell if you are dealing with people like this is to look at their business history. What's their track record with previous employers or business deals? Have they stayed with companies for reasonable periods or have they jumped from job to job like a bullfrog on hot pads? Developing endurance will help build your credibility, expand your opportunities, and improve your résumé.

Bulletproof/Marshmallow at Work

Let's combine high self-confidence and high nurturance to see what this entrepreneur looks like. High-nurturing entrepreneurs have the ability to draw good people with good hearts to their company or organization. They create warm work environments that people love being around.

Many of those who launched dot-coms in the late 1990s were this type of entrepreneur. They had what they thought was a great idea, they wanted to get rich, and they liked people. Recently I was in New York City visiting with a friend who told me about his dot-com experience. Typical for the genre he started with what he thought was a great idea, which was one-hour delivery of videos, pizzas, and other convenience items to customers who ordered online. One hour is not a very long lead time, but when hungry families order a pepperoni pizza, two liters of Coke, and a fun video, they want to see a delivery truck well within sixty minutes. The service aspect could not seem to keep up with the increasing demands for faster delivery. And then there were basic industry challenges. Even without adding the burden of door-to-door delivery, the pizza business had razor-thin profits at just 4 percent.

This dot-com venture—which we will call FastVideoPizza.com—had an interesting constraint, and it would soon play itself out in the business plan. The constraint was that the management team was overly nurturing. When the first round of funding came together, they threw a party and celebrated the kickoff of their company. Caterers delivered delicious food, and everyone had a great time making champagne toasts and speeches about the brave new world of the dot-com and the service industry coming together.

FastVideoPizza.com moved forward, celebrating each and every accomplishment with another party. Everyone had fun, and the company paid for it all. The employees were happy because they were given stock options like candy, and the bonuses were tied to available funding rather than performance. The people at FastVideoPizza.com became even happier—like one big family. The problem was that these high-nurturing people had never run a company before.

As FastVideoPizza.com continued to bleed red ink and finally went broke, what do you think they did? They threw a party. The problem was that their "Turn Out the Lights" party and all the previous events came at the expense of the investors. FastVideoPizza.com went broke because they were nice people who wanted to do good things, but their Marshmallow management style got in the way of success.

If only they had realized that being a little less nurturing and a little more direct in dealing with their issues might have secured their futures and those of their investors. Instead they chose to "love" their people and "love" their business as they continued to go broke. As one of them later recalled, "We had a good time together while it lasted." That is not good enough. The initial round of funding raised $25 million, and all of it was spent, in addition to the funds that they raised for the "bridge fund" that never made it. That's a lot of money to do nothing more than provide an enjoyable place to work with a poor business plan.

The constraints that were in play throughout were devastating to those who counted on them to be better businesspeople, which is why high nurturing that is not balanced by high drive and strong business skills can lead to a great party on the *Titanic*.

Of course every so often in history we see a case where multiple constraints all work together to bring out the absolute worst in someone.

Genghis Khan and Enron

The name itself brought fear to all who heard it. Entire nations fled before his rule and terror. The Great Khan ruled between A.D. 1165 and 1227, and his reign was such that to this day his name calls forth images of death, destruction, and horror. *National Geographic* describes his reign this way: "His daring and charisma draw followers from throughout the region, and he masters rival tribe after rival tribe."

Genghis Khan was the leader to follow. He was charismatic and drew the best of the best warriors to himself. Warriors skilled in the art of war flocked to follow him, and they wanted more than anything to be associated with him and able to travel with him to accomplish the feats of victory for which he was renowned. Those who had contributed the most to his victories would be rewarded with the spoils of war: women, wealth, and slaves. Khan's warriors attained great personal wealth from the many bloody wars won during his reign. In fact, history tells us that the destruction was unbelievable, even for that time period.

> Slashing his way across Central Asia, Genghis crushes the great cities that gleamed in Shah Muhammad's crown. Samarkand, Muhammad's own capital, surrenders to the Mongols. So does Bukhara, a metropolis in what is now Uzbekistan. Genghis is unrepentant. "I am the punishment of God," a Muslim historian later quoted him as saying. "If you had not committed great sins, God would not have sent a punishment like me upon you." A witness took a dimmer view: "They came, they sapped, they burnt, they slew, they plundered, and they departed."

Let's look for a moment at Genghis Khan's makeup.

First, we could say that he was clearly *not* a Flatliner—he was a visionary driven to control as much of the world as he could get his hands on.

Second, he was Bulletproof—his high self-confidence took him straight to the top of the leadership ladder in the world at that time.

Third, he was a Bulldozer who rolled over anything in his path.

Fourth, we could safely say that he was an Iceberg with little regard for others.

Add to all these constraints the lack of one of civilization's greatest forces: a respect for rules. What happens when a person does not follow the rules? What happens when a person has the opportunity to write his own rules? What happens if there is no one to control which rules get written and who enforces the rules? The results produce a ruthless despot who rules whoever he wants in whatever way he wants. And here we find the ancestry of corporate despotism.

Genghis Khan ruled the world through tyranny, and all who wished to prosper came to him and paid him homage. Do we have any modern-day Khans? Jeff Skilling of the Enron debacle might come close. *The greater the personal constraints of the leaders, the greater the impact on the organization.* An article in *Business-Week* provides some profound insights into the personal constraints of Skilling, noting that he "hired some 250 bright young MBAs each year, all desperate to prove themselves so they, too, could hit the jackpot. Around Houston, a Porsche was seen as the Enron company car." A former executive confirmed Skilling's empire-building tactics, recalling his policies of buying employee loyalty with money, while others remember his disdain of typical big business, including a comparison one time of ExxonMobil Corporation to a sprawling and unwieldy "seven mast clipper ship" as opposed to Enron's own "efficient" operations.

See any similarities yet? Let's substitute names and see how it reads:

Jeff Skilling was the leader to follow. He was very charismatic and drew the best of the best executives to himself. Those who were skilled in the art of business flocked to follow him. They wanted more than anything to be associated with him and able to travel with him to accomplish the feats of victory for which he was renowned. They shared in the spoils of conquest, and those who had contributed the most to his victories would be rewarded with the spoils of war: women, wealth, and underlings. Each of the executives attained great personal wealth from the many bloody wars won during his reign. In fact, history tells us that the destruction was unbelievable, even for that time period.

Is the scenario familiar? The personal constraints that played themselves out in Genghis Khan's life are the same ones we see at work in the life of Jeff Skilling. Very high achievement drive, high self-confidence, low nurturing, and low rule respecting are the common traits in both men. The picture of Jeff Skilling that emerges through associates and the wreckage of what transpired is truly a chilling one. Let me give you one more quote from *National Geographic* regarding the great Khan: "And he moved over his enemies without any sense of guilt or remorse."

During Skilling's testimony before a congressional committee, he insisted that he had done nothing wrong and did not understand why he was being called to defend himself. This does not square with the testimony of other employees, many of whom were in positions to know the "stories behind the story."

A *Wall Street Journal* editorial titled "The Enron Verdicts" on May 26, 2006, stated:

> Meanwhile, the damage done from this fraud was terrible: tens of billions of dollars in market value, $2.1 billion in pension obligations, and 5,600 jobs lost in the December 2001 collapse. With each of the guilty verdicts carrying potential penalties of at least five years, Skilling and Lay may well spend more time in prison than Fastow, the fraud mastermind.
>
> By way of comparison, WorldCom CEO Bernie Ebbers is now facing 25 years, John and Timothy Rigas of Adelphia Cable 15 and 20 years, respectively, and Tyco's two top former officials 25 years apiece. That's a pretty impressive cleanup job by the Justice Department and (in the Tyco case) Manhattan District Attorney. The business consensus is that the convictions of individuals—some 30 in the Enron case alone—will do more to deter future corporate crime than anything in Sarbanes-Oxley.

Like many other executives who spend their time sharpening business skills and acumen without giving the same attention to their hidden behavioral land mines, Skilling's personal constraints blew up his empire and cost him dearly. And since "no company can rise above the constraints of its leadership," the constraints of those in positions of leadership will ultimately always impact the company.

It's not my intention to castigate Jeff Skilling. Really he is no different than anyone else who has been hijacked by their constraints. We all carry them to work with us and take them home at night. They won't go away unless we work on them and make them go away. If you aren't working on them, you may be risking more than you know.

20 Personal Constraints and Culture

S teve Gaffney and I were sitting next to each other at a dinner party his company, ITT Corporation, was throwing. ITT is a large, multinational firm in the defense industry. They are very heavily involved in the space industry as well as military support systems, communications, water treatment, electronics, fluids, and a host of other things that would dazzle the mind of any good scientist.

Steve was president of the U.S. Systems Division of ITT, and one of his subsidiary companies was a sponsor for NASCAR. The party was for the NASCAR teams with which they were involved. Steve is a barrel-chested, stocky guy who looks like he's been lifting weights all his life. He leaned over and asked, "So what do you do for NASCAR?"

I was there as a guest of Armando Fitz and Terry Bradshaw with the Navy race team. "Steve, I'm a shrink. My job is making them go faster," I answered. We spent the rest of the evening talking about the impact of individual constraints on group performance.

Changing the Corporate Culture

Months later Steve called me. "Flip, can you do the same things for us that you are doing for NASCAR?" I flew to Colorado Springs with one of our senior staff and met with them to see what we could do.

Steve is a strong team player and team builder. But we could both see areas that needed improving. One thing we noticed was that his division (Systems) was extremely competitive—not just in their drive to beat the outside competition but among themselves as well. We gathered profile data on some of their top people, which revealed some personal tendencies to be especially competitive, low nurturing, and critical. Many of the people within Systems had come out of the military, and they had carried much of that operating philosophy with them. Steve wanted to move the whole organization toward a relational model of teams rather than competitive individuals within a group.

The culture of the Systems Division within ITT was one that reflected the personal constraints of the individuals who made up the leadership of the group. *It was the individual constraints of the leaders that would have to change if the group was to change.* That is the reality for culture change.

So for Steve to accomplish group change, he would have to change some of his own personal constraints. His most significant constraint was that he was not a good listener or nurturer. He scored low on nurturance and high on passion and drive. He was a man in a hurry, and he didn't have time to spend listening to the details of the reports of his people. Being extremely bright can be a handicap if it makes you impatient with people who are slower than you are. Steve's ability to grasp concepts quickly resulted in a constant state of tension and impatience, as his engine was always in overdrive. When someone presented information to him, he would say, "Okay, okay, I got it, I got it"—in an attempt to move "onward and upward." Of course all this did was make the employees more nervous, and they would then try to hurry through their report so they wouldn't slow him down. Fortunately Steve and his team were extremely talented and capable enough—even with their constraints—to keep the company moving forward. *But what could they do if their constraints were identified and broken?*

Steve left the meetings feeling like he got what he needed, but his staff members left feeling they had not presented their ideas fully—they had been hurried through material that they had spent days, and sometimes weeks, preparing. Many times they felt dismissed and not fully heard. Steve knew something wasn't working, but he didn't know exactly what it was. If he could figure out the problem, you could bet on him fixing it.

I told him what it was. "Steve, you scare people when you rush them through their presentations. They get nervous just thinking about it. You are intense, and lots of people get intimidated by that. We have to slow this down, and you have to take the time to listen, ask questions, and let people give you the full picture of what they are seeing. Then you'll build a greater team, and you will be able to go 'faster' (using our NASCAR analogy)."

Steve is a guy who gets it. More than that, he is a man with a great heart. He loves deeply, and he works with zealous passion on things he is committed to. He is committed to his wife, Lynn; to his family; and to his work.

The first thing he did surprised me. He called an "all hands" meeting and told them what he had discovered he had been doing and what he was going to do to change it. "I am going to slow down and listen to you guys. I want to know what you think, and I am going to see to it that you know it. We are going to be the best, and I am going to be the first to change." Those who heard the real message in his speech would have instantly picked up the fact that there was going to be a complete culture change, and he was going before them to start making the necessary changes. He was also saying that as he committed to change, he would expect the same of them. If he was going to lead the charge, then he expected them to go with him. And they did. They followed because he was doing the same things he was expecting them to do.

Building a great team is done by leading a great team. The only way to lead a great team is to do the things that are necessary to achieve greatness. Greatness is a personal thing. You become your best—your absolute best—and those around you will be drawn to it. This is not something that you tell others to do but is instead something that you demonstrate to them. They will get the message because it is a message that we all want to get. Seeing someone be their best makes me want to be my best. That is why I love my wife, our team, our partners, our children, and so many of our clients. It's because they show me a better way to be.

It's not that I need heroes. It's that I want to know that it's possible to be a hero—to be my best and to be able to lead my children and my company. I want those around me to be all they can be because as they become so, we are all the better for it. We can't help it. It's contagious, and it's beautiful.

Steve did what he promised. He learned to listen better and to be more affirming. He is more understanding and patient with others today. He has also been promoted to president of Defense worldwide for ITT along with being made senior vice president of the ITT Corporation. And just so you understand, this is about far more than getting that promotion or raise. Steve will tell you that it is about bringing out the best in his family and his team. Healthy, thriving people create a healthy, thriving culture. Choosing to start with personal change is the greatest mark of a leader.

Changing corporate culture is one thing. But what about changing the culture of a nation?

Exploiting Constraints

Cody Alexander was a young man who didn't like school. He lived in Crockett, Texas, with his parents, Kay and Gerald Alexander, who are two of the best horsepeople in the country. I met Cody in my office, as a patient, when Kay brought him to see me because he wanted to drop out of school.

During our second session, Cody went on and on about how he didn't like school. He was sixteen years old and could get a job as a ranch hand, and he didn't see the sense in school in the first place. I looked at him and said that I agreed with him. Kay was sitting next to him, and the look on her face was pure shock.

Then I offered him a job working on my ranch and managing part of our operation. I told him that I would pay him thirty-five thousand dollars per year but that he had to sign a full-year contract with me, and he couldn't accept the job at that rate and then back out. That was a lot of money for that kind of work, especially at his age.

He jumped at the opportunity. In his unbridled enthusiasm he then asked what he would make the year after that, so he could figure out how his future was looking. Like most kids he had some serious dollar signs in his eyes. I told him that I would pay the going wages for a good ranch hand and that he would have a job with me as long as he wanted if he did good work. He was elated—and his mom was ready to pass out.

He asked, "What kind of wages does a hand get with a year's experience?"

"About $6.50 an hour," I replied. Cody was stunned. "What? That's less than I make the first year. Why does the salary go down?" he asked.

"Well, it's simple, Cody. All I have to do is buy you once, and you have sold your education and future to me for thirty-five thousand dollars. You will have dropped out of school, and you will never be worth that again. But you can't easily go back, and so I have you, for the rest of your life. You're the one who is for sale, and I am the one who is buying. Do we have a deal?"

He looked at me with defiance in his eyes as he said, "You're trying to take advantage of me, and that's not right."

"Actually, son, I'm not trying to take advantage of you. You are being stupid, and I am showing you how I am going to exploit your ignorance. You want to drop out of school, and I am going to make it easy for you to do so. I can use a good hand, and you are a good worker. What's the problem?"

A year and a half later, we received Cody's high-school graduation invitation in the mail. I also got a call telling me that he wanted the job I had offered him earlier. We made a deal at seven dollars an hour. The rest of his request was the best part.

"Can I live with you and Susan while I go to college?"

"Yes, you can, son," I said.

Cody lived with us for five years and went on to complete a masters degree, as well. His parents, Kay and Gerald, and Susan and I are very proud of him. More important, he is proud of himself. He has earned his future when he could have sold it cheaply.

What's my point? Cody's personal constraints of low endurance and low self-control were about to destroy his future. I could have easily exploited those constraints, and he would have paid for it the rest of his life.

Don't think for a minute that there aren't forces at work to keep people personally constrained. It doesn't matter which color or nationality or class or group people come from—all must deal with industries and institutions every day that are designed to work against efforts to break free of addictions like gambling, alcohol, and drugs, even shopping, Internet, and television addictions.

Culture is defined as "the totality of socially transmitted behavior patterns, arts, beliefs, institutions, and all other products of human work and thought" (*American Heritage Dictionary*).

If culture is shaped by the choices of the individuals of that group, then those individual choices will determine the long-term health of that society. The alarming proliferation of pornography and gambling; the glamorization of music and entertainment that is morally degrading to women; comedians who entertain with jokes about the worst of behaviors, such as drug use, lawlessness, racism of all kinds; and violence against others are all warning shots across the bow of our nation for what lies ahead if societal constraints continue to be ignored.

The moral and behavioral choices of individuals will ultimately determine the health of a nation—but what does this have to do with personal constraints?

As goes the individual—so goes the culture—and so goes the nation. With each personal choice we either strengthen the nation or we weaken it. We cannot afford the consequences of living lives devoid of purpose and value. *Our nation suffers greater risk with each poor choice even as we gain strength with each good choice.*

Just as we saw how the culture within ITT's Systems Division reflected the personal constraints of the individuals who made up the leadership of the group, we see a principle that works on any scale: culture change is driven by individual change. If we refuse to address our personal constraints as individuals of a nation, we cannot expect to escape the consequences that follow. There are many areas that we *can* address and changes we *can* make to meet the challenges of our current culture. Remember, the individual behavioral choice is always yours. I watched as Steve Gaffney responded to a challenge to raise the bar and set new standards for excellence in his own life, and those changes are being felt throughout the entire ITT global corporate culture. The company's performance is right behind him—and headed to the top.

And the same principles work for our national culture. If you, and I, and our neighbors, and our children choose to break free from what holds each person back—we will all experience a new freedom to live above our personal constraints.

Our country will be richer for our choices. This is what visionaries like Dr. Martin Luther King and tens of thousands of others have dreamed of and have spent entire lifetimes trying to attain for the next generation. For a nation to be healthy, the people within it must be healthy.

21 Listening to What Others Say: The Power of Honest Feedback

A profound difference exists between *living* a life and *leading* a life. For people to live their lives, they need only to show up each morning and get through the day. For people to lead their lives, they must have direction, purpose, passion, and preparation. Leading your life is living in the fullest sense of the word.

So why do so many simply live their lives "in quiet desperation," not knowing where they are going and what they are doing? First, it takes an honest search to find out who we are and where we want to go in this great journey of life. Second, it takes considerable discipline to get there once you have found out where you are wanting to go. And even though this might sound simple, many people do not make the journey successfully because they don't do the work that it takes to get there.

Feedback: Breakfast of Champions

Most people have never learned to listen very well. Those who *do* listen can't always integrate change and improvement into their behavior.

But those with the ability to listen and integrate—to take change from concept to behavior—will go to the top.

They are learners, and they will outperform those who can't capitalize on new information, methods, or skills.

Many people have said to me, "Flip, I don't really get much feedback."

The reason most people don't get feedback is that *they don't want it.* I have seen my share of people who are difficult to talk to, and they let you know it. They are unapproachable, and the way they carry and present themselves to others raises a deliberate stop sign that shuts down any possibility of dialogue on deeper issues.

But people who do want feedback know how to get it. They seek it out. If you want to be a champion, then you have to eat the right diet. That diet is feedback.

When the Screen Goes Blank

I have a friend I respect greatly. Although he is a very pleasant guy, sometimes his thoughts and emotions don't seem to make it into his expressions. Once I suggested to him that he might want to open up more and express the good feelings he had for others. He looked a little confused at my words. I got more specific.

"Sam, you are difficult to read sometimes because when you are thinking, a scowl settles on your face." Now it isn't a true scowl, but it looks like one from anyone else's view. The truth is that when Sam is thinking, he goes "into the back of his head" and gets caught up in what is going on back there. And when he does, his face goes flat. I told him, "When you are thinking, the screen in front goes dead while you are running the processor in the back of your head. You look angry."

He looked at me in disbelief; he had never heard this before. I asked if we could ask his secretary what she thought. I brought this up because I would have asked Amy (my senior administrator) her opinion about myself, and I know she would have told me what she thought.

Sam was not comfortable doing that, to which I responded, "Then go home and ask your wife what *she* thinks—I'll bet she agrees with me!" Although he was hesitant at first, he loves his wife dearly and so he did, and she did, and that day, Sam began to be more aware of what his face was saying to the world while he was off thinking about important things.

Now when he goes "flat screen," his wife is able to say, "Are you in there? Are you happy?" and he gets the message. Feedback in a trusting relationship makes all the difference in the world.

Using Emotions to Avoid Feedback

There is another group of people who have a way of keeping feedback from coming their way. These are the "criers." When you try to talk to them about something that is uncomfortable for them, they immediately begin to cry. They cry because you have hurt them. You are the perpetrator, and they are the victim. You have done something to them, and they are hurt because of it.

I have found that there are lots of people who use emotions to keep others from giving them feedback. Some will cry, others will yell and get angry, some will withdraw, and then there are the sulkers. But they all use emotions for the same reason: it is effective in making the unpleasantness stop. They don't want feedback because they are unwilling to work through the pain of it, so they find the most effective ways to shut it down as soon as it touches real issues.

Answering to "The Board"

Blue Mondays are only partly descriptive of what NFL players face after a Sunday afternoon of work. It's Black and Blue Mondays. Stiff and Sore Mondays. Bruised and Battered Mondays. Any body part that doesn't hurt is probably still under the influence of painkillers.

Does that sound like a productive setting to have your personal failures hung out in public for all your teammates and coworkers to see?

Probably not, but that was the weekly reality for offensive lineman Anthony Muñoz during most of his thirteen-year career with the Cincinnati Bengals. The fact that he not only accepted this public evaluation of his performance but actually embraced it as a vital—though unpleasant—means of eliminating his constraints is a primary reason he is in the Hall of Fame today.

Not long after he retired from football, I invited Anthony to speak with me at a national education conference. As we visited prior to our session, the conversation turned, as so many of my discussions do, toward what it takes to be the best in any field of endeavor.

Anthony didn't hesitate. A major secret of his success was "The Board."

The stark name communicates tons. This was not something warm and cuddly. It wasn't a fun place to hang out. It was a serious way to deal with serious progress (at least serious in the world of winning football games).

"I dreaded it, especially after a loss," he admitted. "I wanted to be told what a great job I'd done, get a little sympathy for the pain I endured."

On the Monday after each game, before the Bengals escaped to the whirlpool or started studying next week's opponent, they came face-to-face with an unblinking and very graphic reality—a large board with a grid layout. Along the left side of the grid was the name of each player, and in the boxes to the right were quantitative evaluations of his performance on a scale of one to ten. This was not the time or place for general comments or an overall game evaluation. Every player was rated on each play he had been in on the field.

There, in black and white, was precise and authoritative feedback on how each player responded to every opportunity he had been given to be his best—and all of his teammates and coaches could read it, too.

The temptation, naturally, was to check the other guys' scores. What did the wide receiver get when he dropped that pass in the end zone? Did my substitute get top marks while I was out of the game? Did the coaches notice that the guy beside me was loafing?

But the players who really wanted to be the best knew the place to look for success was beside their own names. Anthony was—and still is—very competitive, so his goal was a ten on each and every play. He pushed himself to give his best, studying those numbers and quizzing the coaches for the reasons behind them, not to argue for higher marks but to identify and work on any constraints they revealed.

Former teammate and fellow offensive lineman Max Montoya has noted that Anthony's pursuit of perfection looked a lot like unrelenting hard work. "He played for thirteen years like he was trying to work his way into a starting slot," Montoya said.

Anthony has the size (six feet six inches, 278 pounds) and the skill to have done less than his best and still rate pretty well if he had adopted a "take-me-like-I-am" attitude. Raised by a single mother, he could have resented male authority figures telling him what to do. He could have blamed the occasional poor play on medically challenged knees (three major injuries in four years at USC—yet he missed only three games in thirteen years in the NFL).

Instead he chose to listen and learn—even when the coaches' criticism might have been off target. A prime example was when Bengals line coach Jim McNally insisted the left-handed Muñoz use a right-handed stance. He did as he was told and easily made the all-rookie team. But when McNally reversed himself and let Muñoz go back to the left-handed stance he'd used at USC, the string of all-pro honors was under way.

Similarly he could have ignored "The Board," dismissed the coaches' evaluations as inaccurate, fumed that he was not given the respect due to an all-pro like himself, or made excuses for any low numbers. Instead he embraced the information and used it to get better—and wound up recognized for his greatness.

Muñoz was selected Offensive Lineman of the Year by the NFL Alumni Association four times (1987, 1989–91). His 1989 citation reads: "The NFL has three levels of offensive linemen. The bottom rung is for players aspiring to make the Pro Bowl. The next step is for those who have earned all-star status. Then there's Anthony Muñoz. He's alone at the top."

Fear—The Final Frontier

As a graduate student I was invited to co-present with a colleague at the American Sociological Association Annual Conference in Washington, D.C. Following the discussion a very distinguished gentleman—whose reputation I knew quite well—introduced himself to me and asked if we might visit. He was head of the Department of Sociology of one of the most prestigious universities in the world. As we visited he expressed an interest in what I was working on and then asked, "Would you like to come to our university to complete your doctoral degree? You will study and work with me on an assistantship if you accept the invitation."

It was all I could do to speak. I was standing in the presence of a legend in my field, and he was extending a personal invitation to work with him. It was truly more than I could have ever dreamed of as a twenty-four-year-old student with a long history of learning challenges.

Each of us comes to various crossroads in our lives. We have doors that open and others that close. There is rarely a clear direction, other than what our own values and morals point to. When I began to think about the whole concept of personal constraints, I of course started with my own. I believe we all have personal constraints, and I think they affect us in many ways that we don't even begin to understand. While some are obvious to all, like the knot on Richard's head, others are so deeply hidden that we don't even know they are there or realize the many decisions they actively influence.

From the time I was in the second grade, I have wanted my life to count, to make a difference in the world I live in. I have wanted to grow and fulfill whatever purpose my life holds and to do all that I could to help others grow to fulfill theirs, as well.

Yet I have learned over the years that my own personal constraints were the biggest hindrance to these desires. I began to look at them more closely to understand the connection and impact they were having on my life. If I could discover my personal constraints and work to remove them, then I knew that my life would be different, and I would perform at an entirely new level.

Why am I sharing all this?

Because that day I turned down the offer of a lifetime.

The lesson I learned that day—but did not fully understand until many years later—is that we all tell ourselves stories. In fact, our lives are made up of stories. It is the stories that we tell ourselves that make us who we think we are.

I had a chance to study with one of the greatest intellects of my time in my field, *and I turned him down.*

I had several good reasons for not going, which included the costs of getting ready to go and of actually getting there. Plus too many things needed my attention at home. My reasons made up the story I would tell others so I could explain why I did not take an incredible opportunity. Of course I told myself the same story—and was so convincing, I even believed it. I *had* to believe it, so that I could feel okay about passing up the invitation and all it represented for my future.

We tell ourselves stories so we don't have to deal with the truth when it is painful or hard to face.

So what was the truth? The truth was that *I was afraid of failing.* Still dogged by a deep sense of inadequacy that started early on with my learning disabilities, I could not see my many victories over the years—only the potential for a humiliating defeat. The thought of going somewhere I had never gone before—a prestigious university—only to FAIL was just too much. My failure would expose my deepest fears and ruin my story—although I would then just have to make up a story for why I failed. It might be that it was someone else's fault, or the time wasn't right, or whatever details would make my story sound good.

Years later, when I faced the REAL reason why I had not gone to "that" university, I was disappointed in myself. Not for turning the invitation down, but for allowing my fears to make the decision for me. To be offered an opportunity was one thing, but to go and discover I was as inadequate as I had suspected was another thing entirely. I would rather be able to say I was accepted but that I chose not to go.

I have decided that my fears will not make my decisions for me anymore.

When I am afraid I will choose to face my fears and do whatever it is I am afraid of doing. This, of course, brings me to you, my friend.

What will you do?

Will you look at your own personal constraints and face them or will you decide it is easier to tell yourself a story? The choice is yours.

Did you know that you are born with only two fears? We come into this world with two inborn fears: the fear of falling and the fear of loud noises. *Every other fear we have in life is a learned fear.* Some fears are for our own safety in a highly complex and busy world, while others we picked up along the way in response to imagined threats or one-time threats that no longer exist. Therefore, anything that was picked up along the way can be dropped off at any time you choose.

Refuse to Be Held Back

I have also found that there seem to be only two real reasons for not changing: fear of failing and not caring enough about yourself or others to make the change.

Don't allow fear or apathy to keep you from making the changes you need to make. There are people who count on you. Whether you like it or not, they need you to be all you can be. The question for you is, are *they* worth it? Are *you* worth it? I believe so.

Change takes you to new places.

I watched Mark McCormack change his way of dealing with his family and employees, and it changed his life. Terry Bradshaw changed his way of relating to his race team and got incredible results. Nolan Ryan changed some of his business relationships, and I changed my practice of adopting every new idea that crossed my path. My neighbor changed being focused on getting everything perfect, and one of my sons changed being irresponsible with his money. One of my closest friends is more nurturing now, and countless kids have embraced change for a chance at a different future.

Each and every one of us has personal constraints to break; we just need a plan to know where to start to get the biggest "bang for the buck" in the OPC process.

I don't mind having personal constraints that I need to address— I just don't want to have the same personal constraints *next year* that I had *this year.* I am still growing, but with each step I become more of who I was destined to become.

I am excited about it.

I want to be that person, and I want to celebrate life with others who choose to be all they can be, as well.

I hope that in this journey you, too, discover the life you've always known could be yours.

Conclusion
Raised in Captivity

As you approach our property on the drive to my office, you
can't help but notice a picturesque ranch to your left. Strikingly
peaceful, it is populated by a variety of exotic antelope and deer. The
fence surrounding the property closely parallels the road, so these
animals are a short distance from your car as you drive by. More than
once I've caught myself staring at them when suddenly the rumble of
the gravel alerts me that I've edged off the road.

Like everyone else I appreciate the beauty and grace of these ma-
jestic creatures. But I am more intrigued that, seemingly by common
accord, they accept the artificial boundary imposed by the fence my
neighbor put around them. It's only about four feet high, so even the
yearlings could easily bound over it. But none ever does. Born with
the inherent ability to exceed and escape the barriers constraining
them, something holds them back. Perhaps it's because, raised in cap-
tivity, they've never known anything other than a fenced-in world.
They have the strength and the ability to get out. *They don't have the
vision.*

That fence provides a vivid metaphor for the constraints on human
lives as well. Every day men and women sell short their potential
because of limitations they meekly accept—and often self-impose. I
guarantee that by identifying and addressing personal constraints in
your life, you will enter a whole new world of fulfillment and opportunity—far beyond the fences.

Waiting to celebrate with you (outside the fence),
Flip

Next Steps
Where Do I Go from Here?

At this point hopefully you feel that this book has been beneficial to read. If you enjoyed what you've experienced, I'd like to let you know about some continuing-education opportunities. To learn more about personal and/or organizational growth, you can go to www .flipsidebook.com. We look forward to serving you.

Acknowledgments

How do I say thank you to the many people who have not only helped me with this book but also have helped me grow as a person? There are only a limited number of words that can express it, so to all of them I would like to say, "THANKS." I am better because of you.

I wrote this book because I have the ability to write, and I have read thousands of other books because I also have the ability to read. My teachers made that possible. From my pre-K class in Orange, Texas, through my graduation and ultimately through graduate school, I was taught by people who believed in me. My teachers have given me the ability to do what I do. My heart's desire is to honor them by using what they have given me. Thank you for teaching me and thank you for NOT letting me run away when I wanted to.

I always say that a man is wise when he marries above himself. I did that when I married Susan. She is the air I breathe and the love I hold. She is a saint, and everyone who knows her also knows the impact she has on my life each day. I adore you, Susan. Thank you for seeing more in me than I could see and for nurturing it to fruition. Susan is also a brilliant businesswoman and serves as CEO of our companies.

Dr. Chris J. White (PhD in statistics) is the coauthor of this manuscript. Chris is not only one of my closest friends, but he is brilliant, and much of this work is directly tied to his efforts and thoughts. Chris is the foremost authority on the testing instruments that we have developed to assess personal constraints as well as the best I have ever met at taking executives (or anyone for that matter) through a well-structured personal-growth process. He helped write much of this work, and his hands have closely guarded the entire project.

Next is Ken Abraham, who is truly uniquely gifted in the world of writers. It has been an honor to write with someone of his caliber. I also want to thank Sandy Bloomfield, who worked with us on this project. Sandy and I locked ourselves away in Mellionnec, France, and worked twenty-hour days for an extended period of time to get the manuscript finalized.

I have been blessed with an incredible company and great team to work with. The Flippen Group is the largest teacher-educator company in North America and is filled with awesome people who love teachers and kids. Our work with corporations and other organizations continues to expand as it adds value and enhances cultures. In addition we are one of the fastest-growing executive- and personal-development companies in the country. Our team is the best team I have ever known, and they continue to help me become the best I can be. I love you guys more than you know.

My partner, Lee Bason, is my constant friend and a great source of strength. He is without a doubt one of the most faithful men I have ever known, and he challenges me every day of my life to be better. Lee is one of the best executive consultants I know.

I also want to thank my family for their love and the education they have given me. If a man's wealth is measured in family, I am among the richest of all.

I know that you can write a book without an agent. But can you sell a book without an agent? I don't think I could have done this without Lisa Queen. Lisa, you are tremendous, and I am forever thankful for your encouragement and kindness to me. On top of that, by your introducing me to Springboard Press, I got the privilege of working with Michelle Howry. What a great editor. Thanks for making this book a reality.

Two people in our company have been a tremendous help to me

in this process: Kris Basala and Chad Chmelar. They are extremely talented men who have contributed a great deal to me personally.

Many others have also helped me tremendously in various ways. Amy Wimpee is my right-hand person. Amy runs my office life and is one of our dearest friends. Barbara Knowles has worked with me in various roles for over thirty years and has believed in me even when I questioned what I was doing. Tom Knowles, Barbara's husband, is a well-known author who helped me with various ideas. Steve Tinkle worked with me from the very start of my thoughts about Overcoming Personal Constraints. Steve worked tirelessly on the data programming that served as the basis of our data collection and processing.

Betsy McCormack has become one of our closest friends, and she and Mark opened doors into the sports world that only they had access to. That friendship has been priceless. As a result of that, I got to meet Howard Katz, a great person, who was gracious enough to film a special on our work that was aired during a Super Bowl pre-game show.

Keith Byrom critically and graciously read through the manuscript and offered many thoughts that were valuable during the early phases. Craig Bird, Danelle McAfferty, Mike Yorkey, and Tom Spain also contributed to the early drafts, each helping me think through how best to move forward.

This has been a fun process. I have really enjoyed doing this book with Chris and the team. To all of those friends and associates who have encouraged us along the way: thank you for being there for us.

Last, I want to express my deepest thanks to God for His love and grace in giving me the life and family He has so graciously given me.

Index

About the Authors

FLIP FLIPPEN is a man with an uncompromising mission to build relationships and processes that bring out the best in people. His influence stretches for decades, and the ripples travel across continents. Leading educators, executives, and athletes say his processes help them accelerate personal growth, performance, and productivity. As seen on the *Today* show and the Super Bowl pregame, Flip is a powerful force in the field of growing greatness.

Along with being an internationally renowned speaker and psychotherapist, Flip is also an energetic and successful entrepreneur. He has founded numerous businesses, including The Flippen Group, which stands as the largest educator-training company and one of the fastest-growing leadership-development organizations in North America.

Flip conceived the philosophy of Overcoming Personal Constraints (OPC), which teaches people how to break the constraints that limit their performance and hinder their growth.

Today Flip's innovative processes are at work in the nation's top boardrooms, classrooms, and locker rooms. On the personal side, Flip and his wife, Susan, who reside in College Station, Texas, have a passion for kids and have helped raise more than twenty children.

DR. CHRIS J. WHITE has the uncanny ability to make things simple, operating under the philosophy that if much explanation is necessary, then he hasn't done his job. Highly skilled at applying complex models and thought processes to real-life situations, his mind has gears that never stop turning in his desire to create proven processes that change lives. Armed with numerous university teaching awards and clients that circle the globe, he is a foremost expert in personal coaching and assessment.

Chris; his wife, Jennifer; and their three spunky children reside in College Station, Texas, where he works as director of coaching and development at The Flippen Group.